GENDER, HETEROSEXUALITY, AND YOUTH VIOLENCE

GENDER, HETEROSEXUALITY, AND YOUTH VIOLENCE

The Struggle for Recognition

James W. Messerschmidt

ROWMAN & LITTLEFIELD PUBLISHERS, INC.
Lanham • Boulder • New York • Toronto • Plymouth, UK

Published by Rowman & Littlefield Publishers, Inc.
A wholly owned subsidiary of The Rowman & Littlefield Publishing Group, Inc.
4501 Forbes Boulevard, Suite 200, Lanham, Maryland 20706
www.rowman.com

10 Thornbury Road, Plymouth PL6 7PY, United Kingdom

British Library Cataloguing in Publication Information Available

Library of Congress Cataloging-in-Publication Data
Messerschmidt, James W.
  Gender, heterosexuality, and youth violence : the struggle for recognition /
James W. Messerschmidt.
    p. cm.
  Includes bibliographical references and index.
  ISBN 978-1-4422-1370-8 (cloth : alk. paper) — ISBN 978-1-4422-1371-5 (pbk. :
alk. paper) — ISBN 978-1-4422-1372-2 (electronic)
  1. Youth and violence. 2. Body image in adolescence. 3. Sex differences
(Psychology) in adolescence. 4. Heterosexuality. I. Title.
  HQ799.2.V56M474 2012
  303.60835—dc23

                                                            2012000836

∞™ The paper used in this publication meets the minimum requirements of
American National Standard for Information Sciences—Permanence of Paper
for Printed Library Materials, ANSI/NISO Z39.48-1992.

Printed in the United States of America

For all youth who daily experience
the horrors of bullying victimization

Contents

Acknowledgments

I am forever deeply grateful to Lenny, Kelly, Sam, Kristen, Jerry, and Karen for talking openly with me and sharing their lives—they are the core of this book. Without the cooperation of these six youth, as well as their parents or guardians, this book would have never been written.

Access to the boys and girls interviewed for this project was made possible by a number of people who graciously took time away from their own work to help me. Special thanks to the University of Southern Maine's Institutional Review Board, in particular, ex-associate provost and dean of graduate studies, Margo Wood, for her wonderful help with the consent form, as well as to Virginia Doss, Michael Graff, Tracy Morton, Sheila McKinley, Steve Muslawski, Daniel Nee, and Tina Vermiglio.

As always, the Access and Interlibrary Loan Services librarians at the University of Southern Maine's Glickman Family Library have been an essential component to my research. I thank in particular Loraine Lowell, John Plante, Zip Kellogg, and Pat Prieto.

I also wish to extend considerable appreciation to the entire staff at Rowman & Littlefield, but especially to Sarah Stanton (acquisitions editor), who has graciously and wholeheartedly supported my work over the years, and to Jin Yu (assistant editor), Jehanne Schweitzer (senior production editor), and Brooke Goode (copyeditor).

Most of all, thanks to Ulla, Erik, Jan, and Mel, the most important people in my life!

Finally, parts of this book have appeared elsewhere in a different form. I thank SAGE Publications for permission to reproduce the following: chapters 4 and 6 are revised and expanded versions of "The Struggle for Heterofeminine Recognition: Bullying, Embodiment, and Reactive Sexual Offending by Adolescent Girls." The final, definitive version of this paper has been published in *Feminist Criminology* 6 (3) (2011): 203–33. Copyright 2011 by SAGE Publications, Inc. Reprinted by permission of SAGE Publications, Inc.

1

Introduction

If one empirical observation is unquestionable, it is that the vast majority of those who engage in crime do so with, and through, their bodies. Whenever individuals engage in the harms sociological criminologists label crime, they often use and rely on their bodies to carry out such acts, and this is especially the case for interpersonal violent crimes, such as assault and sexual violence. And regarding specifically the latter, such violence clearly involves embodied *sexual* practices. As Carol Smart (1989: 44) noted over twenty years ago regarding the crime of rape, "you cannot, by fiat, take sex out of a sexual act, it will creep back in at every point." Despite this primacy of the body to crime generally and also of sexuality to sexual violence at least, however, sociological criminologists historically have eschewed an examination of how the body *and* sexuality actually relate to crime and violence. This exclusion of the body and sexuality from sociological criminology is rooted partially in a rejection of nineteenth- and early twentieth-century biological and multifactor perspectives. Sociological criminology emerged by exclusively embracing the social causes of crime as the principal object of theoretical focus—emphasis on the social provided a secure defense against attempts to explain crime as simply epiphenomena of biology. Thus, sociological criminologists adopted a disembodied approach to crime that was distinct from and irreducible to biology. In proclaiming criminology as exclusively a sociological discipline—as, for example, Edwin Sutherland did in the late 1920s and early 1930s (Laub and Sampson 1991)—sociological criminologists historically left to biologists the task of scrutinizing the body and to sexologists the charge of investigating sexuality. Accordingly, in sociological criminology, the body and sexuality—biologically or phenomenologically—were denied any place in the formation of self and crime. Let's look closer at this development and how it is related to sex and gender.

The Origins of Sociological Criminology

Though sociology as an academic discipline developed in France, the United States, Britain, and Germany in the final two decades of the nineteenth century, it nevertheless initially flourished primarily in the United States between 1920 and 1950 (Connell 1997). The focus of sociological knowledge during this time was on internal "social problems" of U.S. society, marked by "the prominence of the Chicago school's urban research and the growth of specializations within sociology" (1536). One such specialization was, of course, criminology.

Edwin Sutherland (1924) published the first sociological textbook on crime, which was intended as a review of the current literature on the causes of crime and on the social control of crime. In his textbook *Criminology*, Sutherland (1924) presented an eclectic multifactor perspective in which he noted that a combination of biological and social conditions affected crime. However, a mere two years after the publication of his first edition, Sutherland rejected biology as an essential component for understanding crime and introduced a perspective that concentrated exclusively on the social. In "The Biological and Sociological Processes," Sutherland (1926: 60) argued that sociological processes are unique and differ from biological processes in that a social act must always be a joint act in which other individuals participate in some way, "and the act of each individual must appear in the act of the other participants." In sociological processes, "[o]ne takes the part of, puts himself [or herself] in the place of, or plays the role of, these others" (60). For Sutherland, the essential characteristic of social processes was social interaction in which the act of each person had meaning to the other person: "Meaning is an objective thing, inhering in the behavior of the participants and in the objects with reference to which they act" (60).

Sutherland (62) pointed out that many sociologists of his time attempted to explain sociological processes by relating them to "the entire universe outside those processes" (such as a combination of sociological, biological, and psychological processes). However, Sutherland now argued against multifactor or "synthetic methods" (as he called them) inasmuch as numerous studies had shown that what earlier had been explained in terms of biological factors could now be articulated more satisfactorily in terms of social interaction: "Thus, at one time crime was explained as due to biological equipment. Now it is rather generally agreed by sociologists that we have practically no explanation of crime in terms of biology" (62). Sutherland maintained that sociology should separate from other disciplines—such as biology—so that a sociology of crime could be effected scientifically: "The most significant reason for the separation of sociology from biology is that it makes possible a limitation of the task of the sociologist so that his [or her] task can be performed scientifically. No science can deal with the entire universe. Nor can any science explain all concatenations of particular events" (64).

John Laub and Robert Sampson (1991) pointed out that during this period Sutherland was developing a form of sociological positivism in which crime was viewed as a social phenomenon that could only be explained by social factors. This is not surprising, as Sutherland was influenced greatly by such members of the Chicago School of Sociology as Robert Park, Ernest Burgess, Louis Wirth, and George Herbert Mead, as well as by Frederick Thrasher's (1927) sociological research on gangs and Clifford Shaw and Henry McKay's (1929) early work on the geographic distribution of delinquency (Gaylord and Galliher 1988). The result was that Sutherland accepted the idea that crime should

be conceptualized exclusively "from the point of view of its relation to the social situation in which it occurs" (Sutherland 1926:
89). Sutherland found in the work of Charles Horton Cooley
the theoretical tools necessary to forgo biology and construct a
sociological perspective that concentrated on social interaction
in particular social situations. For example, in "Social Process
in Behavior Problems" Sutherland (1932: 113) utilized Cooley's
position, concluding:

> The social process by which delinquent behavior develops is
> the same as the social process by which non-delinquent behav-
> ior develops. . . . The variant is not in the social process but in
> the situation. Consequently social process may be a valuable
> step in the explanation of delinquent behavior, but it does
> not in itself contain the explanation of delinquent behavior as
> contrasted with non-delinquent behavior, since the process is
> the same in each.

Sutherland's interaction and interviews with a professional
thief—eventually published in book form in 1937 as *The Professional Thief*—primarily suggested to him what it was that conveyed criminality through social process. As he put it: "I had
worked for several years with a professional thief and had been
greatly impressed by his statement that a person cannot become
a professional thief merely by wanting to be one; he must be
trained in personal association with those who are already professional thieves" (1956: 17).

Consequently, by the end of the 1930s Sutherland (1956: 19)
had concluded that "learning, interaction, and communication
were the processes around which a theory of criminal behavior
should be developed. The theory of differential association was an
attempt to explain criminal behavior in that manner." Indeed, in
the 1939 edition of his textbook—now titled *Principles of Criminology*—Sutherland (1939: 4–5) proposed that "systematic criminal
behavior is determined in a process of association with those who
commit crimes, just as systematic lawful behavior is determined
in a process of association with those who are law-abiding," and it
is this "differential association" that "is the specific causal process
in the development of systematic criminal behavior."

Sutherland bolstered his view that biology has nothing to do directly with criminality by attacking vehemently multifactor approaches that included a biological dimension in their analyses. For example, in their examination of the 1930s debate between Sutherland and Sheldon and Eleanor Glueck, Laub and Sampson (1991: 1404) conclude that Sutherland's adherence exclusively to a social explanation

> resulted in a theory that virtually required him to destroy individual-level, or nonsociological, perspectives on crime. The Gluecks advocated a multi-factor theory of crime, which to Sutherland represented a threat to the intellectual status of sociological criminology. Hence, Sutherland's attack was aimed largely at extinguishing their interdisciplinary model so that sociology could establish proprietary rights to criminology.

Laub and Sampson argue further that "Sutherland became the warrior for sociology's coup of criminology" and viewed rejection of individual factor perspectives (biological, psychological, and multifactor) "as a 'professional turf' concern in making the case for a sociological criminology with himself as its leader" (1421). Indeed, in their detailed treatment of the emergence and development of differential association theory, Mark Gaylord and John Galliher (1988: 137) argue that Sutherland "was quick to jump to sociology's defense whenever he perceived a threat from outsiders. As a master of critical and searching analysis he fulfilled the role of vigilant guardian superbly. As a result he won the unflagging support of his colleagues." Not surprisingly, Sutherland was elected president of the American Sociological Association in 1939.

In Sutherland's final version of differential association theory he presented a perspective that maintained a strict dichotomy between the social and the biological, focusing on the former as defining exclusively the realm of criminological inquiry. In the fourth edition of his textbook published in 1947 (three years before his death), Sutherland listed nine steps in "the process by which a particular person comes to engage in criminal behavior"—establishing crime as a "learned" behavior through interaction with others in intimate personal group settings, and the learning included the techniques of committing crime as well as the motives, drives, rationalizations, and attitudes necessary to engage in crime (Sutherland 1947: 6–7).

The exclusion of the body and sexuality from sociological criminology thus is found partially in the epistemological foundations of differential association theory that are rooted in a rejection of nineteenth- and early twentieth-century biological and multifactor perspectives.[1] Sociological criminology emerged by embracing social interaction and the learning of definitions favorable to lawbreaking as the principal objects of theoretical focus. As Sutherland implicitly claimed as early as 1926, social interaction and the learning of crime need never be reduced to biology; the emphasis on the social provided a secure challenge against attempts to explain crime simply as epiphenomena of biology. Although a laudable intellectual development and thus an important breakthrough in the history of sociological criminology, Sutherland nevertheless adopted a disembodied approach to crime generally and a view of sexual violence that excluded sexuality. In proclaiming criminology exclusively a sociological discipline, then, Sutherland followed the dichotomization of culture and nature—and the Cartesian mind-body split—that developed in sociology generally during this time period (Turner 1996). The focus of sociological criminology was examination of social and cultural processes affecting the mind; it was left to biology to scrutinize the body and to the sexologists to investigate sexuality.[2]

Regarding specifically the sexologists, Richard von Krafft-Ebing (1886), Havelock Ellis (1897), Magnus Hirschfield (1922), and Alfred Kinsey (1948) were pioneers of this intellectual genre. However, it seems that Sutherland was only aware of the work of Kinsey (as he does not cite the others in his published work), which is most likely related to the fact that both Sutherland and Kinsey taught at the same university (Indiana) at the same time. Kinsey and his colleagues published *Sexual Behavior in the Human Male* in 1948, a work based on interviews of some fifty-three hundred men and concluded that a continuity of gradations in male sexual behavior between exclusively heterosexual and exclusively homosexual histories, with bisexuality in the middle, was prevalent in the United States. Kinsey's research then showed that what society considered abnormal (homosexuality) was actually quite common in the male population.

Sutherland (1950) cited Kinsey in one of his papers on sexual psychopath laws, not for the purpose of integrating sexuality into differential association theory but, rather, to belittle psychiatric support for such laws. For example, Sutherland (546) noted the following regarding homosexuality, which was considered a "sex crime" at that time:

> Hundreds of homosexuals can be found in any large city. Few of them are arrested because their perversions are generally limited to their own kind and constitute little danger to the rest of society. Many of these perverts have a good standing in society. Nearly four thousand homosexuals were discharged from the armed forces; they exceeded the average in intelligence and education, and were generally law-abiding and hard working. The Kinsey investigation indicated that more than fifty percent of the males studied, who had arrived at middle age, had had some homosexual experience in their lifetimes.

Although Sutherland shockingly considered homosexuality a "perversion," he cited Kinsey's work to show that homosexuality was not populated by "degenerate sex offenders" and that homosexuals were not a danger to society. What Sutherland left unexplored however was how the Kinsey data may contribute to a conceptualization of sexuality as "learned" through interaction with others in intimate personal group settings. And not surprising, in his discussion of rape Sutherland disregarded how sexuality might play a role in the perpetrators' behavior, instead concentrating exclusively on the alleged behavior of rape victims. As Sutherland (545) states in the same article: women often bring charges of rape for purposes of "blackmail," or simply to "protect their reputations" because they "have engaged voluntarily in intercourse but have been discovered"; "forcible rape is practically impossible unless the female has been rendered practically unconscious by drugs or injury"; "many cases reported as forcible rape have certainly involved nothing more than passive resistance"; and finally, "statutory rape is frequently a legal technicality" because the victim is a prostitute who actually takes "the initiative in the intercourse" and "the preliminary reports of the Kinsey investigation of the sex behavior of the female indicate millions of cases of statutory rape occur annually in the average state." Kinsey and his colleagues published *Sexual Behavior in the Human Female* in 1953, and Sutherland must have seen an early draft. Sutherland then utilized Kinsey's data to blame female victims of rape in order to bolster his argument that official statistics on rape "are useless as an indication of the extent of the danger of serious sex crimes," and thereby in his attempt to challenge the validity of sexual psychopath laws (545). In short, Sutherland's attention to and citation of Kinsey's work was not to integrate sexuality into differential association theory but once again to simply chasten psychiatric support for such laws and thus sustain the ascendancy of sociological criminology (Galliher and Tyree 1985; Gaylord and Galliher 1988).

Although Sutherland's discussion of sexual psychopath laws brushed aside the behavior of sex offenders and exclusively focused attention on the behavior of rape victims, the concentration of his sociological criminology clearly was on boys, men, and crime, as he all but ignored girls, women, and crime. In his textbook, women are omitted altogether and girls are discussed solely in terms of their conformity. For example, in a section on the "sex ratio of crime," girls are depicted by Sutherland as identical—all girls "from infancy" are "taught that they must be nice" and, therefore, they commit very little crime relative to boys (1947: 101). This is the extent of Sutherland's discussion of girls and women. Arguably, Ngaire Naffine (1987: 31) is correct when she states that for Sutherland—as for the vast majority of criminologists during and after him— "Femaleness emerges as an anomaly," and an unequal sex dichotomy was ushered into sociological criminology. Thus, Sutherland (not unlike other sociologists of his time) dislodged boys and men—but not girls and women—from the realm of biology and placed them squarely in the realm of the social. As Anne Witz and Barbara Marshall (2003: 351) put it, an ontology of difference was evoked that rendered "man as social and society as male."

As I have documented in greater detail elsewhere (Messer-schmidt 1993), continuing to the early 1970s the history of sociological criminology is for the most part a history of research and theories written by men and about social man (although not gendered or sexual man). And although sociological criminologists recurrently disregarded women, when women were finally acknowledged, the emphasis in sociological criminology on social man occurred alongside an emphasis on biological woman. Indeed, Cesare Lombroso's *Criminal Woman* was the major influence on conceptions of women and crime from the late 1800s until the early 1970s, primarily because so few sociological criminologists were willing to challenge that perspective (Rafter and Gibson 2004). A prime example that followed in the footsteps of Lombroso is the work of Otto Pollak, who published *The Criminality of Women* in 1950 and who cited favorably Lombroso's conclusions as well as passionately supporting his combined "quantitative and qualitative approach." As a multifactor sociological criminologist, Pollak did acknowledge the influence on women of some social conditions, and he did discuss a few inequalities between men and women as impacting women's involvement in crime. Nevertheless, Pollak's (1950) major argument was that although women's crime most likely equaled that of men's, women's crime was largely "masked criminality." This was so for several reasons that located the primary cause of women's crime in the female body.

First, Pollak argued that women were "addicted" to crimes that were concealed easily, such as shoplifting, prostitute theft, domestic theft, abortion, and perjury. Consequently, the crimes committed by women were more often underreported. Second, women were biologically more deceitful than men and, therefore, more prone to criminal concealment. Pollak stated that this "natural" deceit derived from the biological fact that a man "must achieve an erection in order to perform the sex act and will not be able to hide his failure." Yet for women: "Lack of orgasm does not prevent her ability to participate in the sex act. It cannot be denied that this basic physiological difference may well have a great influence on the degree of confidence which the two sexes have in the possible success of concealment and thus on their character pattern in this respect" (10). Finally, Pollak declared that women concealed menstruation. Thus, the biology of women and its impact on sexuality (for Pollak, intercourse is *the* sex act!) and menstruation made "concealment and misrepresentation in the eyes of women socially required and commendable acts . . . [conditioning] them to a different attitude toward veracity than men" (10). As Pollak (11) concludes: "Almost all criminals want to remain undetected, but it seems that women offenders are much better equipped for achieving this goal than are men." Thus, intercourse was employed to biologize women, and Pollak's *The Criminality of Women* became so popular that it was reprinted numerous times and cited uncritically for the next twenty years (Rafter and Gibson 2004).

Thus, the missing woman in criminology was granted entry into criminological discourse only as the inferior biological woman. Until the early 1970s, sociological criminologists constructed an "essential sex difference" that equated women with "the natural body" and men with "the social mind." Reflecting the presuppositions already in place in U.S. gender relations, sociological criminologists conceptualized the cause of male crime as outside the body and the cause of female crime as inside the body. Thus, the rise of sociological criminology rested on the culture-nature, mind-body, and social man-biological woman binaries. Consequently, in sociological criminology the female body remained "Other": biologically enigmatic, afflicted, deceitful, and, therefore, in need of pervasive social control by men. Indeed, Sutherland, Pollak, and other sociological criminologists were not dissimilar from sociologists in general, who, prior to the 1970s, developed a "masculine ontology of social being." Sociology as an academic discipline—and resultantly sociological criminology— emerged through a process whereby "women are locked into and overwhelmed by their corporeality, whilst men rise above it and are defined, determined and distinguished by their sociality" (Witz and Marshall 2003: 351).

Feminist Criminology

Second-wave feminism was stimulated by Simone de Beauvoir's well-known argument in *The Second Sex*: "One is not born but rather becomes a woman." As de Beauvoir pointed out: "biological fate" does not "determine the figure that the human being presents in society; it is civilization as a whole that produces this creature indeterminate between male and eunuch which is described as feminine" (1972: 295). De Beauvoir argued that the social—not the biological—determines women's situation; that is, women are embedded socially in unequal patriarchal gender relations where they are compelled "to assume the status of Other" (29). Indeed, it is not biology that determines women's destiny, "but the manner in which her body and her relation to the world are modified through the action of others than herself" (734).

The Sex-Gender Binary

Despite de Beauvoir's tremendous influence, it was Ann Oakley who eventually made a more thoroughgoing distinction between "sex" and "gender" in her book *Sex, Gender, and Society* (1972). Oakley defined "sex" as the biological differences between men and women (genitalia and reproductive capacities that are allegedly universal and immutable) and "gender" as the social differences associated with each sex ("masculinity" and "femininity" that are variable and culturally mutable). Thus, in confronting the culture-nature and social man–biological woman binaries, second-wave feminists created a new binary, an offshoot of the mind-body dualism—the sex-gender distinction.

Equipped with de Beauvoir's analysis of women's oppression in patriarchal society and Oakley's sex-gender binary, feminist sociological criminologists redefined women's condition—and thus involvement in crime—in social rather than in biological terms. As Nicole Hahn Rafter and Frances Heidensohn (1995:

3) pointed out in their discussion of the development of feminist perspectives on crime, the distinction between "sex" and "gender" made clear that "gender subordination was neither inborn nor inevitable. Once made, the sex-gender distinction enabled feminists to break free of crippling roles and eventually to imagine cultures in which sexual and gender identities might be mixed, matched, and even multiplied."

Early feminist criminologists of the second wave then shifted the analysis of women and crime—as Sutherland had done for men and crime—from biological determinism to social determinism; from the body to the mind. For feminists there is nothing distinctive about women's biology that causes women's subordination; rather, inequality between men and women is a socially learned and gendered phenomenon that can be socially unlearned and, therefore, changed. Indeed, throughout the 1970s and into the 1980s, feminist sociological criminologists concentrated on criticizing criminological theory for being gender-blind, for misrepresenting women, and for being unable to account sociologically for women and crime. As Eileen Leonard (1982: 1–2) concluded after an exhaustive analysis of criminological theory:

> Theoretical criminology was constructed by men, about men. It is simply not up to the analytical task of explaining female patterns of crime. Although some theories work better than others, they all illustrate what social scientists are slowly recognizing within criminology and outside the field: that our theories are not the general explanations of human behavior they claim to be, but rather particular understandings of male behavior.

Structural Feminist Criminology

Following this development, three differing structural feminist theories of crime emerged in the 1980s—marxist feminism, radical feminism, and socialist feminism—to explain crime by women and men as well as violence against women. All three theories reproduced the mind-body and sex-gender binaries and thus none of these theories included any discussion of the body. Moreover, marxist feminism had little to say about sexuality while radical and socialist feminism for the first time attempted to place sexuality on the criminological agenda. Let me discuss one criminological example for each of the above feminist perspectives that developed during this time period.

Marxist feminists theorized, following Engels (1970), that the class and gender divisions of labor together determine the social position of women and men in any society, but they see the gender division of labor as resulting from the class division of labor. According to marxist feminists, as private property evolved, males began to dominate all social institutions. Thus marxist feminists viewed the capitalist mode of production as the basic organizing mechanism of Western societies; this mode of production determines the social relations between classes and genders. Gender and class inequalities result from property relations and the capitalist mode of production. In addition, marxist feminists viewed masculine dominance as an ideological manifestation of a class society in which women are primarily dominated by capital and only secondarily by men. The latter form of domination, however, results from the mode of production. Although most marxist feminists examined masculine dominance and sexism in society, they comprehend the roles of men and women in relation to capital, not in relation to a separate system of masculine power and dominance. Women's labor in the home is analyzed not in terms of how it benefits men but, rather, how it provides profits for the capitalist class.

An excellent illustration of a marxist feminist perspective in 1980s feminist sociological criminology is Julia and Herman Schwendinger's (1983) book, *Rape and Inequality*. The Schwendingers contend that the level of male violence in any society is determined primarily by class relations and the mode of production, and that societies without commodity production are gender egalitarian, women are deemed equal to men in most aspects of social life, and violence against women is almost nonexistent. When such societies begin to produce for exchange (either voluntarily or because of the imposition of colonial power), men control the production system and women are confined to the home. This new division of labor results in an increase in male authority, a decrease in women's social position, and violence against women. Hence, gender inequality and violence against women become closely tied to and rooted in the mode of production. The Schwendingers argued that exploitative modes of production in class societies either produce or intensify gender inequality and violence against women, because in such a society masculinity has become linked with violence and femininity with nonviolence, and all citizens perceive these stereotypes as natural. According to the authors, this "sexual fetishism of violence," along with men's contemptuous attitudes toward women leads, under capitalism, to violence against women (197–207). Needless to say, both the body and sexuality are completely unexplored in this marxist feminist account and the sex-gender distinction was solidly maintained in this theoretical formulation.

Whereas marxist feminism emphasized the structural conditions of a class society (more specifically, a capitalist society) as the root cause of masculine dominance, gender inequality, and thus crime, radical feminism examined masculine power and privilege as the root cause of all social relations and inequality. For radical feminists, the most important relations in any society are found in "patriarchy" (masculine control of the labor power and sexuality of women); all other relations (such as class) are secondary and derive from male-female relations. Radical feminists also assert that heterosexuality is a form of structural power, "and gender, as socially constructed, embodies it, not the reverse" (Stanko 1985: 73). Thus, an essentialist view of heterosexuality emerges in radical feminism as the structural foundation upon which gender is socially practiced.

An example of radical feminism in 1980s feminist criminology is Elizabeth Stanko's (1985) book *Intimate Intrusions,* in which she claims that because of masculine dominance and female powerlessness in society, the "normal" male is physically aggressive and the "normal" female experiences this aggression in the form of heterosexual violence. For Stanko, violence against women seems to be universal across time and place: "To be a woman—in most societies, in most eras—is to experience physical and/or sexual terrorism at the hands of men" (9). Thus, male violence is a reflection of the universality of male dominance and the secondary status of women. Moreover, Stanko argued that such male dominance values women's sexual purity and men's sexual prowess, which become the defining features of "normative heterosexuality." Consequently, "women learn, often at a very early age, that their sexuality is not their own and that maleness can at any point intrude into it. . . . As such, male sexual and physical prowess takes precedence over female sexual and physical autonomy" (73).

Stanko goes on to point out that under such conditions of male heterosexual power women are considered first and foremost sexual beings and, therefore, "women's sexuality is treated as if it were essentially available to any man within any setting" (74). The result is that women, as appendages to men, are "expected to endure or alternatively have been seen as legitimate, deserving targets of male sexual and physical aggression because that is part of what men *are*. Women, as connected to men, are then violated" (74). Male heterosexual violence is customary in patriarchal culture; therefore, it is also customary that women endure it. Thus, normative heterosexuality helps maintain male dominance and control over women. As Stanko concluded: "Forced sexuality for women is 'paradigmatic' of their existence within a social sphere of male power" (75).

Finally, socialist feminism differed from both marxist and radical feminism: It prioritized neither class nor sexuality nor gender. Socialist feminists viewed primarily both class and gender relations as interacting and co-reproducing each other in society. For socialist feminists, class and gender interact to determine the social organization of society at any particular time in history. To understand class, socialist feminists argue that we must recognize how it is structured by gender; conversely, to understand gender requires an examination of how it is structured by class. Consequently, people's overall life experiences are shaped by both class and gender relations, and the interaction of these relationships structure crime in society.

An example of a socialist feminist explanation of crime is my book *Capitalism, Patriarchy, and Crime* (Messerschmidt 1986). In

this work I argued that the United States is a patriarchal capitalist society and that the interaction of patriarchy and capitalism
patterns the types and seriousness of crime. This interaction
creates a powerless group of women and the working and
lower classes, on one hand, and a powerful group of men and
the professional-managerial (traditional middle) and capitalist
classes on the other. Arguably then, power constituted by both
gender and class is critical to understanding crime:

> It is the powerful (in both the gender and class spheres) who do
> most of the damage to society, not, as is commonly supposed,
> the disadvantaged, poor, and subordinate. The interaction of
> gender and class creates positions of power and powerlessness
> in the gender/class hierarchy, resulting in different types and
> degrees of criminality and varying opportunities for engaging
> in them. Just as the powerful have more legitimate opportuni-
> ties, so they have more illegitimate opportunities (42).

Given that men and members of the professional-managerial
and capitalist classes have the most power, they have greater opportunities to engage in crime, not only more often but also in
ways that are more harmful to society. Males of all social classes
therefore commit more crime than females, their class position
determining the type of crime they may commit (for example,
lower- and working-class males have no opportunity to commit
corporate crimes, whereas professional- and managerial-class
males have no need to resort to conventional crimes), and low
female crime rates are related to women's powerless position in
the United States. Their subordinate position relegates women
to fewer legitimate as well as fewer illegitimate opportunities
and to fewer resources with which to engage in serious forms
of crime. Thus, overall, socialist feminists argue that crime is
related to the opportunities a gender/class position allows, and
they attempt a simultaneous explanation of the gender and class
patterns of crime.

In this work I integrated sexuality into my socialist feminist theory when specifically discussing heterosexual violence
against women. For example, I argued that in patriarchal capitalism "normative heterosexuality" involves a "presumption that

men have a special and overwhelming 'urge' or 'drive' toward heterosexual intercourse," and consequently they are (134):

> expected not only to be sexual but to exhibit to other males their sexual prowess. A man who views women as sex objects rather than full human beings associates his masculinity with "how much he gets." Women come to be, to these men, justifiable objects of sexual exploitation. . . .Thus, some men see violent sexual situations as legitimate behavior—the culture of patriarchal capitalism tends to legitimize rape.

Although both radical and socialist feminism were the first to attempt to integrate heterosexuality into sociological criminology, they eschewed any analysis of the body and its relation to both heterosexuality and crime and they simultaneously maintained the sex-gender binary. And regarding specifically heterosexuality, radical and socialist feminists were only partially successful: both theories examined heterosexuality at the structural level, refraining from any analysis of heterosexuality as a social practice and how heterosexual identities are constructed and maintained through everyday interaction. Heterosexuality and its relation to violence against women by men was theorized as resulting exclusively from a structural system—"patriarchy" or "patriarchal capitalism"—external to the social actor. For these two theories, then, individuals display little or no creativity: their actions simply result from the structural conditions of "the system." Both radical and socialist feminism failed to account for the intentions of actors and how everyday social practices, including both sexuality and crime, are situationally and meaningfully *embodied* constructs in themselves. Thus, sexuality as "structured social action" remained essentially unexplored as a theoretical question.

Contemporary Feminist Criminology

Notwithstanding, as feminist criminology was about to move into the 1990s, Kathleen Daly and Meda Chesney-Lind (1988: 108) outlined what they considered to be the five core elements of feminist thought that should guide feminist criminological research and theory building, yet none of their declared elements included the body or sexuality and therefore maintained the mind-body and sex-gender binaries:

1. Gender is not a natural fact but a complex social, historical, and cultural product; it is related to, but not simply derived from, biological sex difference and reproductive capacities.
2. Gender and gender relations order social life and social institutions in fundamental ways.
3. Gender relations and constructs of masculinity and femininity are not symmetrical but are based on an organizing principle of men's superiority and social- and political-economic dominance over women.
4. Systems of knowledge reflect men's views of the natural and social world; the production of knowledge is gendered.
5. Women should be at the center of intellectual inquiry, not peripheral, invisible, or appendages to men.

Assuming a "natural" sex dichotomy in society, feminist criminologists have employed these elements of feminist thought to conduct investigations of women's gendered lives and experiences in terms of primarily race, class, and age. Second-wave feminist criminologists challenged the masculinist nature of criminology by illuminating the patterns of gendered power that, to that point, sociological criminology had all but ignored. In particular, feminist criminologists secured a permanent role for feminism in criminology and moved analysis of gendered power and social woman (alongside social man) to the forefront of much criminological thought. To be sure, since the 1990s feminist scholars have spotlighted and thoroughly researched (1) the nature and pervasiveness of violence against women, (2) girls' and women's crimes and the social control of girls and women, and (3) women working in the criminal justice system (e.g., Belknap 2006; Chesney-Lind and Pasko 2004; Chesney-Lind and Irwin 2007; Chesney-Lind and Jones 2010; Daly and Maher 1998; Maher 1997; Martin and Jurik 2007; Miller

2001, 2008). The importance of this feminist work is enormous. It has contributed significantly to the discipline of criminology and has made a lasting impact—the gravity of gender in understanding the differences and similarities in crime by men and women is acknowledged more broadly now and has become a permanent feature within the discipline.

Moreover, the second-wave feminist criminological turn to gender not only illuminated sociological issues unknown previously about women, crime, and social control, it has led also, logically, to the critical study of masculinity and crime. Boys and men are seen no longer as the "normal subjects"; rather, the social construction of masculinities has come under careful criminological scrutiny. In recent years there has emerged a new and growing sociological interest in the relationship among men, masculinities, and crime. Since the 1990s, numerous works have been published, from individually authored books (Messerschmidt 1993, 1997, 2000, 2004, 2010; Polk 1994; Collier 1998; Winlow 2001; Mullins 2006; Tomsen 2009), to edited volumes (Bowker 1998; Newburn and Stanko 1994; Sabo, Kupers, and London 2001; Tomsen 2008), to special academic journal issues (Carlen and Jefferson 1996). This development makes perfect sense because if gender is conceptualized in terms of power relations, it becomes necessary to study not simply the powerless but also the powerful. As with any structure of power and inequality (such as race and class), it is essential to study the powerful. Indeed, the gendered practices of men and boys raise significant questions about crime. Men and boys dominate crime. Arrest, self-report, and victimization data reflect that men and boys perpetrate more conventional crimes—and the more serious of these crimes—than do women and girls. Moreover, men have a virtual monopoly on the commission of syndicated, corporate, and political crime. To be sure, criminologists have consistently advanced gender as the strongest predictor of criminal involvement. Consequently, studying masculinities provides insights into understanding both the highly gendered ratio of crime and crime by individuals in society. Thus, among criminologists interested in gender and crime, what have emerged are studies examining differences in crime between women and men based on gendered woman (femininities) and gendered man (masculinities).

Nevertheless, conceptualizing a relationship between social and gendered processes and crime—although an important and essential theoretical development within sociological criminology—has caused a disadvantageous aftereffect that has prompted sociological criminologists (feminist and nonfeminist alike) to perpetuate the mind-body binary by ignoring how those who engage in crime (both men and women) interact with and through their bodies. Both feminist and nonfeminist sociological criminologists established (at different times) and continue to maintain (in different ways) specific types of perspectives on crime in which the body is completely untheorized, as the concentration for the most part is on the gendered mind. Consequently, there has developed an inevitable reluctance by sociological criminologists to incorporate in their theories aspects of human embodiment.[3]

Sociological criminology generally rejected the body as a domain for theoretical and empirical enquiry, yet from the very beginning of second-wave feminism the body became a political issue as women struggled to gain control over their bodies. Recent academic feminist empirical and theoretical work *outside* criminology has addressed, for example, how men and women experience their bodies, how men's and women's bodies are implicated in various social and cultural practices, symbolic representations of men's and women's bodies, and how cultural discourses shape men's and women's embodied experiences (e.g., Davis 1997; Morgan and Scott 1993; Lorber and Moore 2007; Crawley, Foley, and Shehan 2008).

Although feminist criminologists have also extensively shown the ways in which girls' and women's bodies are exploited, harmed, and dominated under unequal gender relations, they have never confronted how gender and sexuality are embodied. As Judith Allen noted in 1989, feminist criminologists have criticized criminology's historically inadequate analysis of the causes of women's and men's crimes, yet they have endorsed simultaneously the mind-body and sex-gender binaries. This endorsement positively enabled a move to conceptualizing gendered woman and gendered man, yet use of these binaries removed any link between the body and gender; indeed, any notion of the socially constructed "gendered and sexual body" has been rendered arbitrary. Although the sex-gender distinction allowed feminist criminologists to investigate women's and men's social and gendered experiences without reverting to biological determinism, for these feminists gender was constructed socially but the body and sexuality were not.

Consequently, feminist criminologists have, as have sociological criminologists generally since Sutherland, "constructed the body as fixed, immutable, static and utterly outside culture" (Allen 1989: 34). Feminist and profeminist criminologists historically have neglected how social action, lived experience, sexuality, and crime/violence, are embodied. Not only have feminist and profeminist criminologists concentrated on gender differences in crime—thereby ignoring possible gender similarities in crime—they have also conceptualized the body and sexuality as "natural" phenomenon that lie outside their analytical concerns.[4] Indeed, the concept of gender did not wholly erase "sex" from the feminist agenda, since feminist scholars—as noted above— argued that gender is *related* to, but not simply *derived* from, sex. Feminist criminologists have refuted continually and soundly any claim that gender is derived from sex, yet they have never confronted the important question: If sex does not play a causal role in gender, how exactly then is gender related to sex?[5] Moreover, despite the important insights by radical and socialist feminist criminologists, theorizing heterosexuality did not become central to feminist criminology. Thus, for feminist criminologists, "gender" is constructed socially, but "sex" and "(hetero)sexuality" are not. Accordingly, "sex" and "(hetero)sexuality" have remained undertheorized within feminist criminology. Let me then close this chapter with a brief reconsideration of the historical relationship among "sex," "gender," and "sexuality."

Revisiting Sex, Gender, and Sexuality

In historical studies on the definition of "sex" and "sexuality," gender has proved always to be already involved. The work of Thomas Laqueur (1990) is exemplary in this regard, and in his important book *Making Sex*, he shows that for two thousand years a "one-sex model" dominated scientific and popular thought in which male and female bodies were not conceptualized in terms of difference. From antiquity to the beginning of the seventeenth century, male and female bodies were seen as having the same body parts, even in terms of genitalia, with the vagina regarded as an interior penis, the vulva as foreskin, the uterus as scrotum, and the ovaries as testicles. Women thus had the same body as men but the positioning of its parts was different: as one doggerel verse of the period stated, "women are but men turned outside in" (4). Thus, in the "one-sex model" the sexes were not seen as different in *kind* but rather in *degree*— woman simply was a lesser form of man. And as Laqueur (8) explains, "*Sex*, or the body, must be understood as the epiphenomenon, while *gender*, what we would take to be a cultural category, was primary or 'real.'" Inequality was imposed on bodies from the outside and seen as God's "marker" of a male and female distinction. To be a man or a woman was to have a specific place in society decreed by God, "not to *be* organically one or the other of two incommensurable sexes. Sex before the seventeenth-century, in other words, was still a sociological and not an ontological category" (8).

What emerged after the Enlightenment was a "two-sex model" involving a foundational dichotomy between now two and only two distinct and opposite sexes, as no longer did scientific and popular thought "regard woman as a lesser version of man along a vertical axis of infinite gradations but rather an altogether different creature along a horizontal axis whose middle ground was largely empty" (148). Indeed, in Michel Foucault's (1980: vii) well-known discussion of the "hermaphrodite" (what is referred to today as the intersexed), *Herculine Barbin*, he shows that by the mid-1800s there was no allowance for any human being to occupy a "middle ground" through "a mixture of two sexes in a single body," which consequently limited "the free choice of indeterminate individuals" and thus henceforth "everybody was to have one and only one sex." Individuals accepted previously as representatives of the "middle ground" ("hermaphrodites") were now required to submit to expert medical diagnosis to uncover their "true" sex. As Foucault (vii) continues:

> Everybody was to have his or her primary, profound, determined and determining sexual identity; as for the elements of the other sex that might appear, they could only be accidental, superficial, or even quite simply illusory. From the medical point of view, this meant that when confronted with a hermaphrodite, the doctor was no longer concerned with recognizing the presence of the two sexes, juxtaposed or intermingled, or with knowing which of the two prevailed over the other, but rather with deciphering the true sex that was hidden beneath ambiguous appearances.

Arguably, then, under the "two-sex model" it became commonplace to view *the* male sex and *the* female sex as "different in every conceivable aspects of body and soul, in every physical and moral aspect—An anatomy and physiology of incommensurability replaced a metaphysics of hierarchy in the representation of woman in relation to man" (Laqueur 1990: 5–6).

Predictably, these two now fixed, incommensurable, opposite sexes also are conceptualized as *the* source of the political, economic, and cultural lives of men and women (gender and sexuality), since "biology—the stable, ahistorical, sexed body—is understood to be the epistemic foundation for prescriptive claims about the social order" (6). To be sure, it was now understood as "natural" that women are, for example, passive, submissive, and vulnerable; and men are, for example, active, aggressive, and perilous. And given that anatomy is now destiny, a heterosexual instinct to procreate proceeds from the body and is "the natural state of the architecture of two incommensurable opposite sexes" (233).

Nevertheless, the term "heterosexuality" actually did not appear until the 1890s, and then it was used to specifically designate an identity based on sexual desire for the opposite sex. Heterosexuality was now disconnected from procreation and "normal" sexuality was henceforth defined as heterosexual attraction; "abnormal" sexuality was homosexual attraction. Thus the concept of heterosexuality was defined in terms of its relationship to the concept of homosexuality, both terms categorizing a sexual desire unrelated to procreation, and individuals now began to define their sexual identity according to whether they were attracted to the same or the opposite sex (Seidman 2010). And Steven Seidman (158) articulates well the historically constructed close connection between gender and heterosexuality:

> There can be no norm of heterosexuality, indeed no notion of heterosexuality, without assuming two genders that are coherent as a relationship of opposition and unity. If there were no fixed categories of gender, if there were no "men" and "women," there could be no concept of heterosexuality! So, heterosexuality is anchored by maintaining a gender order through either celebrating and idealizing gender or by stigmatizing and polluting gender nonconformity.

The shift in thinking to a "two-sex model," consisting now of two different types of humans with complementary heterosexual natures and desires, corresponded to the emergence of the public/private split: It was now "natural" for men to enter the public realm of society and it was "natural" for women to remain in the private sphere. Explaining these distinct gendered spaces was "resolved by grounding social and cultural differentiation of the sexes in a biology of incommensurability" (Laqueur 1990: 19). In other words, "gender" and "sexuality" became subordinated to "sex" and biology was now primary: *the* foundation of difference and inequality between men and women.

Laqueur makes clear that the change to a two-sex model was not the result of advances in science, inasmuch as the reevaluation of the body as primary occurred approximately one hundred years before alleged supporting scientific discoveries appeared. And although anatomical and physiological differences clearly exist between male and female bodies, what counts as "sex" is determined socially. In short, natural scientists had no interest in "seeing" two distinct sexes at the anatomical and concrete physiological level, "until such differences became politically important" and "sex" therefore became "explicable only within the context of battles over gender and power" (10–11).

The historical work of both Laqueur and Foucault suggests that "sex differences" do not naturally precede "gender and sexual differences." And as Wendy Cealey Harrison (2006) insightfully observes, it is virtually impossible to ever entirely separate the body and our understanding of it from its socially determined milieu. Arguably, what is now necessary is a reconceptualization of "the taken-for-grantedness of 'sex' as a form of categorization for human beings and examining the ways in which such a categorization is built" (43).

Outline of the Book

The discipline of sociological criminology historically has maintained, in various ways, the mind-body, sex-gender, and gender difference binaries as well as a one-dimensional structural interest in (hetero)sexuality. Satisfactory research and theory on sex, gender, sexuality, and youth violence requires therefore not simply a rejection of these binaries, but a specific concentration on (1) embodiment as a lived aspect of sex, gender, and sexuality; (2) both differences and similarities in the commission of violence by boys and girls; (3) how embodied social action is embedded in specific structural sex, gender, and sexual relations in particular settings; and (4) how sex, gender, and sexuality are socially constructed through interaction and thus situationally related to crime and violence. It is to these important matters that we turn our attention in the following chapters.

Chapter 2 further expands structured action theory (Messerschmidt 1993, 2000, 2004) by more thoroughly integrating sexuality—or specifically, heterosexuality—into the theoretical equation. The chapter highlights the "doing" of sex, gender, and sexuality, how such doing is related to structural conditions situationally, and how reflexivity involves the negotiation of structural circumstances and individual agency. Chapter 2 also includes a full discussion of the methodology used in the study.

Individuals who have read my preceding books associated with this study—*Nine Lives* and *Flesh and Blood*—will immediately notice that the current book uses several previously discussed life histories but that it introduces some new life stories as well. In chapters 3, 4, and 5, I examine six life histories of three boys and three girls, equally involved in assaultive violence, sexual violence, and nonviolence. What is distinct about this current book is that *all* of the six youth were victims of severe and consequential forms of bullying in school, and then each eventually committed either reactive assaultive or sexual violence, or they remained nonviolent. The individual life stories shockingly demonstrate a social process involving movement from bullying victimization to involvement in violence or nonviolence by each of the six youths. Thus, while these chapters include some recognizable life histories, the analysis is entirely new by offering a unique comparative examination of that social process.

Finally, chapter 6 concludes the book with a discussion of some additional new and compelling findings in the study as well as suggestions of social policies that may be implemented to help curb school bullying and reactive forms of violence.

Let us now turn our attention to a detailed consideration of the theory and methodology used in the study.

2

Theory and Method

The mystery regarding the relationship among sex, gender, sexuality, and differences and similarities in crime ultimately is not hidden inside the fleshiness of the body but, rather, it is readily understood from the outside, luminously flaunted in our socially embodied practices, interactions, and institutions. As Jean-Paul Sartre (1956: 729) would have put it: There is a mystery, but it is "a mystery in broad daylight." Thus, I argue in chapter 2 that the mystery of the relationship among embodied gender, sexual, and criminal practices can be revealed by conceptualizing this relationship as a form of "structured action." In examining life-history data on assaultive violence, sexual violence, and nonviolence by both boys and girls—as I do in chapters 3, 4, and 5—*structured action theory* will provide the means to investigate (1) embodiment as a lived aspect of sex, gender, and sexuality; (2) adolescent gender and sexual practices by both boys and girls; and (3) how such embodied actions may be related to violence and nonviolence. Accordingly, chapter 2 begins with a close examination of the distinctive components of structured action theory, and then, in the following section, I outline the methodology used to gather the data for the adolescent-life stories presented in chapters 3, 4, and 5.

Structured Action Theory

Structured action theory has been employed previously (Messerschmidt 1993, 2000, 2004) in understanding the relationship between gender and crime, in particular masculinities and crime. However, here I expand the theory to conceptualize "doing" sex, gender, and sexuality.

Doing Sex, Gender, and Sexuality

Reflecting various theoretical origins (Connell 1987, 1995; Giddens 1976, 1984; Goffman 1963, 1972, 1979; Kessler and McKenna 1978; Sartre 1956; West and Fenstermaker 1995; West and Zimmerman 1987), structured action theory emphasizes the construction of sex, gender, and sexuality as situated social, interactional, and embodied accomplishments. In other words, sex, gender, and sexuality grow out of embodied social practices in specific social structural settings and serve to inform such practices in reciprocal relation.

Regarding "sex," and as discussed in chapter 1, historical and social conditions shape the character and definition of "sex" (social identification as "male" or "female"). Sex and its meanings are given concrete expression by the specific social relations and historical context in which they are embedded. In an important work, Suzanne Kessler and Wendy McKenna (1978) argue that social action is constructed through taken-for-granted assumptions, or what they call "incorrigible propositions." Our belief in two objectively real, biologically created constant, yet opposite, sexes is a telling, incorrigible proposition. We assume there are only two sexes; each person is simply an example of one or the other. In other words, we construct a sex dichotomy in which no dichotomy holds biologically, historically, cross-culturally, and contemporaneously (Messerschmidt 2004).

The key process in the social construction of the sex dichotomy is the active way we decide what sex a person is (Kessler and McKenna 1978: 1–20). A significant incorrigible proposition of this sex attribution process is that men have penises and women do not. Thus we consider genitals the ultimate criterion in making sex assignments; yet, in our daily interactions we continually make sex attributions with a complete lack of information about others' genitals. Our recognition of another's sex is dependent upon the exhibit of such bodily characteristics as speech, hair, clothing, physical appearance, and other aspects of personal front—through this embodied presentation we "do" sex and it is this doing that becomes a substitute for the concealed genitalia.

Nevertheless, "doing gender" (West and Zimmerman 1987) entails considerably more than the "social emblems" representing membership in one of two sex categories. Rather, the social construction of gender involves a situated social, interactional, and embodied accomplishment. Gender grows out of social practices in specific settings and serves to inform such practices in reciprocal relation. Although sex category defines social identification as "male" or "female," "doing gender" systematically corroborates that sex identification and category through embodied social interaction. In effect, there is a plurality of forms in which gender is constructed: we coordinate our activities to "do" gender in situational ways (West and Zimmerman 1987).

Accordingly, early gender development in childhood occurs through an interactive process between child and parents, other children, and other adults. By reason of this interaction with others, children undertake to practice what is being preached and represented. Raewyn Connell defines the proactive adoption of specific embodied gender practices as the "moment of engagement," the moment when an individual takes up a project of masculinity or femininity as his or her own (1995: 122). The young child has in effect learned to locate himself or herself in relation to others within a sexed and gendered social field (Jackson 2007). Children negotiate the embodied gender practices that are prevalent and attributed as such in their particular milieu(s) and, in so doing, commit themselves to a fundamental project of gender self-attribution—"I'm a boy" or "I'm a girl." This fundamental gender project is the primary mode by which individuals choose to relate to the world and to express oneself in it. Indeed, what makes us human is the fact that we construct ourselves by making reflexive choices that transcend given circumstances and propel us into a future that is defined by the consequences of those choices. Doing gender is a continuing process in which individuals construct patterns of embodied presentations and practices that suggest a particular gender in particular settings and, consequently, project themselves into a future where new situations are encountered and subsequently new reflexive choices are made. Thus, there exists unity and coherence to one's gender project in the sense that we tend to embody this particular sexed and gendered self—"I'm a boy" or "I'm a girl"—over time and space.

Nevertheless, and although individuals construct a fundamental project as either male or female, the actual accomplishment of gender may vary situationally—that is, gender is renegotiated continuously through social interaction and, therefore, one's gendered self may be fraught with contradictions and diversity in gender strategies and practices. Indeed, individuals may situationally adopt cross-gender strategies and engage in certain masculine and feminine practices without changing their fundamental gender project; others may construct a specific fundamental gender project (for instance, masculine) that contradicts their bodily sex category (female).

"Doing" sexuality[1] encompasses the same interactional processes just discussed for "doing gender" and therefore likewise involves children initially acquiring knowledge primarily about heterosexuality through interaction with mothers, fathers, other children, and other adults. This initial process involves the acquisition of mostly nonerotic forms of heterosexual knowledge, such as male-female marital relationships that suggest this is "where babies come from." However, in order to adopt such rudimentary heterosexual knowledge, "doing gender" must take primacy, as Stevi Jackson and Sue Scott (2010: 91–92) point out:

> We recognize someone as male or female before we make assumptions about heterosexuality or homosexuality; we cannot logically do otherwise. The homosexual/heterosexual distinction depends upon socially meaningful gender categories, on being able to "see" two men or two women as "the same" and a man and a woman as "different."

Once children begin to develop a sense of the erotic aspects of sexuality—which usually occurs through interaction with peers in secondary school—"their sense-making is governed by their gendered self—their embodied gendered being" (Jackson 2007: 10). To be sure, "doing" sex, gender, and sexuality intersect here, so that our conceptualization of sex and gender impacts our understanding and practice of sexuality (both the erotic and nonerotic aspects), and it is through sexual practices (once again both the erotic and nonerotic) that we validate sex and gender. Individuals adopt embodied sexual practices as a "moment of engagement," a moment when the individual begins to take up a sexual project affixed to their gender project, constructing for example, heteromasculine and heterofeminine identities. Sex, gender, and sexuality are produced and reproduced by embodied individuals, and interaction with others is essential to one's ability to negotiate and fit into ongoing and situationally constructed patterns of sex, gender, and sexuality.

Crucial to this negotiation and "fitting in" is the notion of "accountability" (West and Zimmerman 1987). Accountability refers to individuals who configure and orchestrate their embodied actions in relation to how such actions may be interpreted by others in the particular social context in which they occur. In other words, in their daily activities individuals attempt to be identified bodily as "female" or "male" through gender and sexual practices. Within social interaction, then, we encourage and expect others to attribute to us a particular sex category. And we facilitate the ongoing task of accountability through demonstrating that we are male or female by means of concocted practices that may be interpreted accordingly. The specific meanings of sex, gender, and sexuality are defined in social interaction and therefore through personal practice. Doing gender and sexuality renders social action accountable in terms of available gender and sexual practices appropriate to one's sex category in the specific social situation in which one acts. Thus, it is the particular gender and sexual relations in specific settings that give behavior its sexed, gendered, and sexual meanings.

In this view, then, although we decide quite early in life that we're a boy or a girl and later we adopt an identity as straight, gay, lesbian, bisexual, etc., the actual everyday "doing" of sex, gender, and sexuality is accomplished systematically and is never a static or a finished product. Rather, people construct sex, gender, and sexuality in specific social situations. In other words, people participate in self-regulating conduct whereby they monitor their own and others' embodied social actions. This perspective allows for innovation and flexibility in sex, gender, and sexuality construction—and the ongoing potentiality of normative transgression—but also underscores the ever-present possibility of any sexed, gendered, and sexual activity being assessed by co-present interactants. Sex category serves as a resource for the interpretation of situated social conduct, as co-present interactants in each setting attempt to hold accountable behavior as female or male; that is, socially defined membership in one sex category is used as a means of discrediting or accepting gender and sexual practices. Thus, although we construct ourselves as male or female, we situationally embody gender and sexuality according to our own unique experiences, and accountability attempts to maintain congruence among sex, gender, and sexuality; that is, male = masculinity = sexually desires females, and female = femininity = sexually desires males.

Moreover, sex, gender, and sexuality construction results from individuals often—but not always—considering the content of their social action and then acting only after internal deliberation about the purpose and consequence of their behavior. *Reflexivity* refers to the capacity to engage in internal conversations with oneself about particular social experiences and then decide how to respond appropriately. In reflexivity we internally mull over specific social events and interactions, we consider how such circumstances make us feel, we prioritize what matters most, and then we plan and decide how to respond (Archer 2007). Although we internally deliberate and eventually make such reflexive choices to act in particular ways, those choices are based on the situationally available sex, gender, and sexual practices. Notwithstanding that sex, gender, and sexuality simply may be a habitual and routine social practice (Martin 2003), accountability encourages people to do sex, gender, and sexuality appropriate to particular situations. And accountability and thus reflexivity especially come into play when individuals are confronted with a unique social situation—such as a challenge to their sex, gender, or sexuality. Nevertheless, the resulting reflexive social action may not actually have been consciously intended to be a sex, gender, or sexuality practice.

Relations, Structures, and Reflexivity

As the foregoing indicates, although sex, gender, and sexuality are "made," so to speak, through the variable unification of internal deliberations and thus reflexive self-regulated practices, these embodied practices do not occur in a vacuum. Instead, they are influenced by the social structural constraints we experience. *Social structures*, defined as regular and patterned forms of interaction over time that constrain and channel behavior in specific ways, "only exist as the reproduced conduct of situated actors" (Giddens 1976: 127). However, social structures are neither external to social actors nor simply and solely constraining. On the contrary, structure is realized only through embodied social action, and social action requires structure as its condition. "Knowledgeable" human agents of gender and sexual practices enact social structures by reflexively putting into practice their structured knowledge; yet, in certain circumstances they may improvise or innovate in structurally shaped ways that significantly reconfigure the very structures that shaped them (Giddens 1984). Because people do sex, gender, and sexuality in specific social situations, they reproduce and sometimes change social structures. And given that people often reproduce gender and sexual ideals in socially structured specific practices, there are a variety of ways to do them. Within specific social settings, however, particular forms of gender and sexual practices are available, encouraged, and permitted. Accordingly, gendered and sexual *agency* must be viewed as reflexive, embodied structured action—what people, and therefore bodies, do under specific social structural constraints (Messerschmidt 1993, 1997, 2000, 2004).

The key to understanding the maintenance of existing gendered and sexual social structures is the accomplishment of such practices through reflexive embodied social interaction.

Social actors perpetuate and transform social structures within the same interaction; simultaneously, these structures constrain and enable gendered and sexual social action. The result is the ongoing social construction of gender and sexual relations. As Abby Peterson (2011) shows, it is in reflexivity where we find the mediatory processes whereby structure and action are linked. Structured action theory, then, emphasizes that it is through reflexive internal deliberations about the constraints and enabling aspects of social structures that people ultimately develop characteristic strategies for handling situations in which gender and sexual relations are present. Social structures influence practice so that some gender and sexual strategies are more successful than others. Accordingly, and as noted earlier, there is likely to be a degree of social standardization of individual gendered and sexual lives—we consistently over time and space construct ourselves as "a boy" or as "a girl" with a particular sexual orientation.

Power, Difference, and Similarity

Power is an important structural feature of gender and sexual relations. Socially organized power relations among men and women are constructed historically on the basis of gender and sexual preference. In other words, in specific contexts some men and some women have greater power than other men or other women; some sexualities have greater power than other sexualities; and the capacity to exercise power and do gender and sexuality is, for the most part, a reflection of one's place in gender and sexual relations of power. Consequently, in general heterosexual men and women exercise greater power than do gay men and lesbians; upper-class men and women exercise greater power than do working-class men and women; and white men and women exercise greater power than do racial minority men and women. Power, then, is a relationship that structures social interaction not only between men and women but among men and among women as well. Nevertheless, power is not absolute and at times may actually shift in relation to different axes of power and powerlessness.

Raewyn Connell's (1987, 1995) concept of "hegemonic masculinity" is relevant here. Initially, Connell conceptualized *hegemonic masculinity* as the form of masculinity in a given historical and society-wide setting that structures and legitimates hierarchical gender relations between men and women, between masculinity and femininity, and among men. The relational character was central to her argument, embodying a particular form of masculinity in hierarchical relation to a certain form of femininity and to nonhegemonic masculinities. Connell emphasized that hegemonic masculinity has no meaning outside its *relationship* to "emphasized femininity"—and to nonhegemonic masculinities—or to those femininities practiced in a complementary, compliant, and accommodating subordinate relationship with hegemonic masculinity. And in the *legitimation* of this relationship of superordination and subordination the meaning and essence of both hegemonic masculinity and emphasized femininity are revealed. This emphasis on hegemony in gender relations underscored the achievement of hegemonic masculinity largely through cultural ascendancy—discursive persuasion—encouraging all to consent to, coalesce around, and embody such unequal gender relations.

Notwithstanding considerable favorable reception of the concept of hegemonic masculinity, it nevertheless attracted such criticisms as (1) concerns over the underlying concept of masculinity itself; (2) lack of specificity about who actually represents hegemonic masculinity; (3) whether hegemonic masculinity simply reduces in practice to a reification of power or toxicity; and (4) the concept's unsatisfactory theory of the masculine subject. Having successfully responded to each of these criticisms, Connell and Messerschmidt (2005) reformulated the concept in appropriately significant ways.

First, they discussed what must be retained from the original formulation, clearly noting that the relational idea among hegemonic masculinity, femininity, and nonhegemonic masculinities, as well as the conception that this relationship is a pattern of hegemony—not a pattern of simple domination—have well withstood the test of time. Also well supported historically are the seminal ideas that hegemonic masculinity need not be the commonest and/or the most powerful pattern of masculinity in a particular setting and that any formulation of the concept as simply constituting an assemblage of "masculine" character traits should be thoroughly transcended.

Second, Connell and Messerschmidt nevertheless suggested that a reformulated understanding of hegemonic masculinity must incorporate a more holistic grasp of gender hierarchy that recognizes the agency of subordinated groups as much as the power of hegemonic groups and that appreciates the mutual conditioning (intersectionality) of gender with such other social dynamics as class, race, age, sexuality, and nation. Moreover, Connell and Messerschmidt asserted that a more sophisticated treatment of embodiment in hegemonic masculinity was necessary, as well as conceptualizations of how hegemonic masculinity may be challenged, contested, and thus changed.

Finally, Connell and Messerschmidt argued that instead of recognizing simply hegemonic masculinity at only the society-wide level, scholars should analyze empirically existing hegemonic masculinities at three levels: *local* (constructed in arenas of face-to-face interaction of families, organizations, and immediate communities); *regional* (constructed at the society-wide level of culture or the nation-state); and *global* (constructed in such transnational arenas as world politics, business, and media). Obviously, links among these levels exist: global hegemonic masculinities pressure regional and local hegemonic masculinities, and regional hegemonic masculinities provide cultural materials adopted or reworked in global arenas and utilized in local gender dynamics.

In addition to the above, the relationship between hegemonic masculinity and emphasized femininity underpins what has become known as *heteronormativity*, or the legal, cultural, organizational, and interpersonal practices that derive from and reinforce taken-for-granted assumptions that there are two and only two naturally opposite and complementary sexes (male and female), that gender is a natural manifestation of sex (masculinity and femininity), and that it is natural for the two opposite and complementary sexes to be sexually attracted to each other (heterosexuality). In other words, the social construction of sex differences intersects with the assumption of gender and sexual complementarity, or the notion that men's and women's bodies are naturally compatible and thus "made for each other"—*the* "natural" sex act involves vaginal penetration by a penis (Jackson and Scott 2010). Heterosexuality is understood culturally as the natural, erotic attraction to sex/ gender difference and thus it reinforces hegemonic masculinity and emphasized femininity as natural and complementary opposites (Schippers 2007). Heteronormativity therefore refers to "the myriad ways in which heterosexuality is produced as a natural, unproblematic, taken-for-granted, ordinary phenomenon" (Kitzinger 2005a: 478). Thus, gender hegemony and sexual hegemony intersect so that both masculinity and heterosexuality are deemed superior, and femininity and homosexuality are judged to be inferior. The social construction of men and women as naturally different and complementary sanctions heterosexuality as *the* normal and natural form of sexuality and masculine men and feminine women as *the* normal and natural gender presentation; any sexual or gender construction outside of these dichotomies is considered abnormal. Heteronormativity then reproduces an unequal sexual binary—heterosexuality and homosexuality—that is dependent upon the alleged natural sexual attraction of two and only two opposite and complementary sexes and in turn constructs masculine and feminine difference. Nevertheless, some heterosexual practices are more powerful than other heterosexual practices; that is, normative heterosexuality determines its own internal boundaries as well as marginalizing and sanctioning sexualities outside those boundaries.

The salience of gender and sexual relations is important because, although both gender and sexual construction are ubiquitous, the significance of gender and sexuality shifts from context to context: in one situation, both gender and sexuality may be important; in another, gender but not sexuality may be significant; and in still other situations, sexuality may be more important than gender. In other words, gender and sexuality are not absolutes and are not always equally significant in every social setting in which individuals participate.

Structured action theory is not a general theory of crime because gender and sexuality vary in salience by social situation. Nevertheless, social relations of gender and sexuality—like class, race, and age—variously join us in a common relationship to others: we share gendered and sexual structural space. Consequently, common or shared blocks of gendered and sexual knowledge about interpersonal practices evolve through interaction in which particular gender and sexual ideals and activities differ in significance. Through such interaction, gender and sexuality become institutionalized, permitting, for example, men and women to draw on such existing but previously formed ways of doing or practicing gender and sexuality to construct particular strategies for specific settings. The specific criteria of gender and sexuality thus are embedded in the social situations and recurrent practices by which gender and sexual relations are structured. Nevertheless, accountability to gender and sexuality are not always, in every social situation, critical to the interaction and thus to the social construction of crime. Thus, I emphasize in this book certain *localized* social situations in which gendered and sexual practices are variably salient to the commission of violence and nonviolence by white working-class adolescent boys and girls.

In addition to gender and sexual hegemony, structured action theory identifies at least four distinct masculinities and femininities: dominant, dominating, subordinate, and equality. "Dominant" masculinities and femininities differ from hegemonic masculinities and emphasized femininities in that they are not always associated with and linked to gender hegemony but refer fundamentally to the most celebrated, common, or current form of masculinity and femininity in a particular social setting. "Dominating" masculinities and femininities are similar to dominant masculinities and femininities but differ in the sense that they involve commanding and controlling specific interactions and exercising power and control over people and events—"calling the shots" and "running the show." Dominant and dominating masculinities and femininities do not necessarily legitimate a hierarchical relationship between men and women, masculinity and femininity. Although hegemonic masculinities and emphasized femininities at times may also be dominant or dominating, dominant and dominating masculinities and femininities are never hegemonic or emphasized if they fail culturally to *legitimate* unequal gender relations. However, dominant and dominating masculinities and femininities necessarily acquire meaning only in relation to other masculinities and femininities (see Beasley 2008; Messerschmidt 2008, 2010).

"Subordinate" masculinities and femininities refer to those masculinities and femininities situationally constructed as lesser than or aberrant and deviant to hegemonic masculinity or emphasized femininity as well as to dominant/dominating masculinities and femininities. Depending upon the particular context, such subordination can be conceptualized in terms of, for example, race, class, age, sexualities, or body display/ behavior. Given the discussion above, it should be obvious that one of the most significant forms of subordination is that of gay boys/men and lesbian girls/women—the former are culturally feminized and the latter, culturally masculinized. In a gender hegemonic culture, then, gayness is socially defined as the embodiment of whatever is expelled from hegemonic masculinity, and lesbianism is the embodiment of whatever is expelled from emphasized femininity. Related to this, a second form of subordination usually occurs if there is incongruence within the sex-gender-heterosexuality structure. For example, girls and women perceived as female who construct bodily practices defined as masculine, such as expressing sexual desire for girls ("dyke"), acting sexually promiscuous ("slut"), presenting as authoritarian, physically aggressive, or take charge ("bitch"), are viewed as polluting "normal" and "natural" hegemonic gender and sexual relations and often are verbally, socially and physically bullied as subordinate and thus repressed (Schippers 2007). Similarly, individuals perceived as male but who construct practices defined as feminine, such as sexually desiring boys or simply practicing celibacy ("fag"), being passive, compliant, or shy ("sissy"), and/or being physically weak or unadventurous ("wimp"), likewise are seen as polluting "normal" and "natural" hegemonic gender and sexual relations and often are verbally, socially, and physically bullied as subordinate and thus repressed (Schippers 2007). Structured unequal gender and sexual relations then are sustained in part through the repression of such "subordinate" genders and sexualities. Subordination can also occur amongst individuals that construct situationally accountable masculinities and femininities. For example, the masculinity of a son may be judged to be subordinate to the masculinity of his father, and the femininity of a daughter may be considered subordinate to the femininity of her mother. Both of these are subordinate primarily by reason of age, not because of any incongruence between sex and gender, and usually are established in relation to dominant/dominating masculinities and femininities.

Finally, "equality" masculinities and femininities are those that legitimate an egalitarian relationship between men and women, between masculinity and femininity, and among men and women. Such masculinities and femininities do not assume a normal and natural relationship to sex and sexuality and usually they are not constructed as naturally complementary.

Gender and sexual practices operate as "on-hand" resources (developed from embodied social actions themselves) available to be actualized into practice in a range of different circumstances. They provide a conceptual framework that is materialized in the design of social structures and, therefore, materialized in daily practices and interactions. Structured action theory permits investigation of the different ways men and women experience their everyday worlds from their particular positions in society and how they relate to other men and women; the embodied gender and sexual practices are associated with the specific context of individual action and are for the most part self-regulated—through reflexivity—within that context. In other words, social actors self-regulate their behavior and make specific reflexive choices in specific contexts. In this way, then, men and women construct varieties of gender and sexuality through specific embodied practices. And by emphasizing diversity in gender and sexual construction, we achieve a more fluid and situated approach to our understanding of embodied genders and sexualities.

Embodiment

As I have emphasized, constructing gender and sexuality entails embodied social practices—reflexive structured action. Indeed, it is only through our bodies that we experience the social world, and the very possibility of a social world rests upon our embodiment (Crossley 2001). As Iris Marion Young (1990: 147–48) points out:

> It is the body in its orientation toward and action upon and within its surroundings that constitutes the initial meaning-given act. The body is the first locus of intentionality, as pure presence to the world and openness upon its possibilities. The most primordial intentional act is the motion of the body orienting itself with respect to and moving within its surroundings.

We understand the world from our embodied place in it and our perceptual awareness of situational surrounding space. The body is a sensuous being—it perceives, it touches, and it feels; it is a lived body. And given that consciousness consists of perceptual sensations, it is therefore part of the body and not a separate substance (Crossley 2001). The mind and the body are inseparably linked—a binary divide is a fiction—and live together as one in the social construction of gender and sexuality. In this conceptualization, then, the body forms the whole of our being and, thus, one's reflexive gendered and sexual "self" is located in the body, which in turn acts, and is acted upon, within a social environment. Indeed, in contemporary industrialized societies the body is central to the social construction of self (Giddens 1991). A proficient and able body is necessary for social action and, therefore, embodied discipline is fundamental to the competent social agent: "It is integral to the very nature both of agency and of being accepted (trusted) by others as competent" (100).

Goffman's (1963, 1972, 1979) important work on behavior in public settings is relevant here, demonstrating how the body actually is the medium by which individuals become active participants in daily life. In particular, Goffman (1963) argues that situationally embodied forms of communication (what he calls "body idioms" and what have been labeled here as "gendered and sexual practices") guide our perception of "appropriate" bodily appearances and behaviors and, therefore, serve as situational constraints. In this sense, then, bodies in our immediate social situations construct, in part, the knowledge we use to act in those situations. Meaning inheres in the explicit appearance and behavior of bodies, which are publicly available through our participation in social interaction. As Crossley (2001: 17) states: "We can only meet and interact with others in virtue of our embodiment, as meeting and interacting are sensuous acts, dependent both upon the sensory systems required to perceive others and the sensible qualities that allow one to be perceived—not to mention the motor capacities required for communication."

Through embodied social action individuals do gender and sexuality while simultaneously presenting such practices as resources for others as a consequence of their embodiment. The social situations in which embodied actions are oriented "are populated by others and it is these others, in part, towards whom the actions are oriented. Action is other oriented" (Crossley 1995: 141). Embodied social action is "interwoven with the perceptual field of the agent," so that what we actually conceptualize are social situations that require specific "practical accommodation from our action"—we reflexively respect, acknowledge, reproduce, and sometimes resist situational embodied conventions (136). And as Goffman (1979: 6) acutely observes, such embodied actions are situational forms of "social portraiture" in which individuals convey information that "the others in the gathering will need in order to manage their own courses of action—which knowledgeability he [or she] in turn must count on in carrying out his [or her] own designs." Doing gender and sexuality therefore is necessarily both reflexive and physical; it is intelligent and meaningful but it also involves "physical doings"—movement through space and physical engagement with other physical beings (Crossley 2001).

Bodies then are active in the production and transmission of intersubjective gendered and sexual meanings, and embodied social actions "are executed in accordance with the others who populate the (intermundane) space of their exercise"; that is, embodied practices "are articulated with the behavior of others" (Crossley 1995: 146). The meaningfulness of our social action is based on the reaction of others to our embodiment—whether or not it is judged accountable is highly important to our sense of self. Embodied accountability is vital to an individual's situational recognition as a competent social agent. If an individual's embodied appearance and practice is categorized by others as "failed," that degradation may result in a spoiled self-concept (Goffman 1968). Consequently, adequate participation in social life depends upon the successful presenting, monitoring, and interpreting of bodies.

Goffman helps us understand how doing or practicing gender and sexuality are intersubjective (because they are intercorporeal) in the sense that we accomplish both bodily and in a manner that is acceptable to situationally populated others. Individuals exhibit embodied gender and sexual competence through their appearance and by producing situationally appropriate "behavioral styles" that respond properly to the styles produced by others. In other words, "competent" individuals develop an embodied capacity to provide and to read depictions of gender and sexuality in particular settings, and appropriate body management is crucial to the smooth flow of interaction essential to satisfactory attribution and accountability by others. To be "read" by others as male, female, masculine, feminine, straight, gay, lesbian, etc., individuals must ensure that their proffered selves are maintained through situationally appropriate display and behavior—the body is social and social settings are created through intercorporeality.

But in addition, properly accountable bodies construct gender and sexual relations; they signal and facilitate through their appearance and action the maintenance of gender and sexual power relations. To be sure, suitably adorned and comported bodies constitute the "shadow and the substance" of unequal gender and sexual relations (Goffman 1979: 6): "The expression of subordination and domination through the swarm of situational means is more than a mere tracing of symbol or ritualistic affirmation of social hierarchy. These expressions considerably constitute the hierarchy; they are the shadow and the substance." Individuals produce (and at times challenge) structured gender and sexual relations through their embodied appearance and actions.

Thus, the body is an essential part of gender and sexual construction in which we fashion appearance and actions to create properly and situationally adorned and performed bodies. The body is an inescapable and integral part of doing gender and sexuality, entailing social practice that constantly refers to bodies and what bodies do; it is not social practice reduced to the body (Connell 2000). Constructing gender and sexuality involves a dialectical relationship in which practice deals with the biological characteristics of bodies: "It gives them a social determination. The connection between social and natural structures is one of practical relevance, not causation" (Connell 1987: 78). In the social construction of gender and sexuality, then, bodily similarities between men and women are negated and suppressed, whereas bodily differences are exaggerated. For example, early adolescent girls are generally physically bigger and stronger than boys their age, yet that bodily characteristic is subdued as enormous social pressure is often, but clearly not always, applied to construct girls as dependent and fearful in comparison to boys.

Nevertheless, bodies participate in social action by delineating courses of social conduct: bodies are agents of social practice and, given the context, will do certain things and not others. Our bodies constrain and facilitate social action and therefore mediate and influence social practices. The body is lived in terms of what it can "do" and the "consequence of bodily practice is historicity: the creation and transformation of situations. Bodies are drawn into history and history is constituted through bodies" (Connell 1998: 7). In short, the body is a participant in the shaping and generating of social practice. Consequently, it is impossible to consider human agency—and therefore crime and violence—without taking gendered and sexual embodiment into account.

Challenges

Nevertheless, certain occasions present themselves as more effectively intimidating for demonstrating and affirming embodied gender and sexuality. In certain situations individuals may experience body betrayal and be identified by others as embodying gender and/or sexual "failure." The constitution of gender and sexuality through bodily appearance and performance means that gender and sexual accountability is vulnerable when the situationally appropriate appearance and performance are not (for whatever reason) sustained. Because the taken-for-granted gender and sexuality of individuals can be challenged in certain contexts, gender and sexuality are particularly salient. They are, as David Morgan (1992: 47) would put it, "more or less explicitly put on the line," and the responding social action can generate an intensified reflexivity and a distinct type of gender and/or sexual construction. Such gender and sexuality challenges are contextually embodied interactions that result in gender and/or sexual degradation—the individual is constructed as a gendered and/or sexually "deviant" member of society. Gender and sexual challenges arise from interactional threats and insults from peers, teachers, parents, workmates, and from situationally and bodily defined gender and sexual expectations that are not achievable. Such challenges, in various ways, proclaim a man or boy, or a woman or girl, subordinate in contextually defined embodied terms. Gender and sexual challenges may motivate social action toward specific situationally embodied practices that attempt to correct the subordinating social situation, and various forms of crime and violence can be the result (Messerschmidt 1993, 1997, 2000, 2004). Given that such interactions question, undermine, and/or threaten one's gender and/or sexuality, only contextually "appropriate" gender and sexual embodied practices can help overcome the challenge. The existence of gender and sexual challenges alerts us to the transitory and fleeting nature of gender and sexual construction, and to how crime and violence may arise as gendered and/or sexual practices when they are regularly threatened and contested.

Social action is never simply an autonomous event but is amalgamated into larger assemblages—what is labeled here as embodied gender and sexuality projects. The situational ideals of gender and sexuality encourage specific lines of social action, and social structures shape the capacities from which gender and sexuality projects are constructed over time. Men and boys and women and girls reflexively negotiate the situations that face them in everyday life, and in the process pursue a gender and sexuality project. From this perspective, then, social action is often—but not always—designed with an eye to one's gender and sexual accountability individually, bodily, and situationally. Structured action theory, then, permits us to explore how and in what respects gender and sexual embodied practices are constituted in certain settings at certain times, and how embodied gender and sexual practices relate specifically to interpersonal violence and nonviolence.

The study in which structured action theory is applied in this book examines the construction and formation of gender and sexual practices through violent or nonviolent social action as one aspect of certain individual embodied gender and sexual projects. Structured action theory is used to explore the ways adolescent-embodied gender and sexual practices are constructed through interaction within the particular social context of specific "sites," such as home, school, and street. In short, to understand working-class adolescent violence and nonviolence, we must appreciate how structure and action are woven inextricably into the ongoing reflexive activities of "doing" embodied gender and sexual practices.

A Theorized Life History

This study investigates adolescent perpetrators of interpersonal assaultive and sexual violence in the context of their entire lives, from their earliest memories to the point at which I encountered them. Such life-history accounts lead to an understanding of the stages and critical periods in the processes of violent and nonviolent gender and sexual development, and to an understanding of how the particular individual is both enabled and constrained by structural position. Criminology reports very little about the life histories of violent adolescent offenders and especially little about when, and under what type of social conditions, they may also be nonviolent. This study is unique in that it explores the similarities between boys and girls and the role of the gendered and sexual lived body in the practice of assaultive and sexual violence or nonviolence. Additionally, criminology historically has been haunted by (but has never addressed adequately) the question of why boys and girls who grow up simultaneously in the same or similar social milieu progress in different yet similar directions throughout the course of their lives.

The present study, then, seeks to understand certain boys' and girls' use of assaultive and sexual violence as gendered and sexual practices. The chief questions of the study are: Why is it that some boys and girls engage in assaultive violence and some in sexual violence, and how are these violent boys and girls similar and different? How are gender and sexual relations in specific settings—such as the family, the school, and the street—related to motivation for embodied violence and nonviolence by these same boys and girls? This differential use of violence is examined as a resource for "doing gender and sexuality" in certain situations and under specific circumstances. To comprehend what it is about adolescent boys and girls that motivates some to commit assaultive or sexual violence, we must comprehend the social construction of gender and sexuality—how assaultive and sexual violence may be meaningful gendered and sexual constructs and embodied practices in themselves and in particular settings. To understand adolescent assaultive and sexual violence, then, we must bring actively and reflexively gendered and sexual subjects solidly into the research picture.

The primary goal is to glean considerable and telling information from a modest sample of white working-class boys and girls who engaged in assaultive and sexual violence and nonviolence. By scrutinizing each detailed life history, we shall begin to learn the social processes involved in becoming violent or nonviolent in certain settings. I believe the study has several significant strengths. First, the boys and girls I interviewed reflect the serious (dark) end of the delinquent behavior continuum and represent a type of offender about whom criminologists must genuinely be concerned: assaultive and sexually violent adolescent males and females. Here *assaultive offenders* are boys and girls from fifteen to eighteen years of age who acted in a nonsexual, physically violent way against at least one other person; there exists no official records of them committing any other type of violent act (e.g., homicide and/or rape) and they all denied engaging in any other type of violence, although they may have committed such other nonviolent crimes as property and drug offenses. Thus, in terms of violence, these boys and girls are exclusively assaultive offenders. The *sexual offenders* I interviewed are boys and girls from fifteen to eighteen years of age who, by coercion or manipulation, engaged in sexual contact (e.g., fondling and/or penetration) with individuals legally unable to give informed consent. All the boys and girls I interviewed were exclusively sex offenders; that is, they denied engaging in any other type of crime and had no official record of committing any other type of crime. The *nonviolent* boys and girls I studied are fifteen to eighteen years of age who had not admitted committing, nor been formally charged with committing, a violent act, or admitted engaging in violence (but were never formally charged) for a brief period early in their lives (and at a young age) and thereafter adopted an exclusively nonviolent pattern of behavior. In structuring these three categories, then, I studied boys and girls who engaged in two different types of violence and their peers who were exclusively nonviolent.

Second, the study includes both boys and girls matched according to the following demographic characteristics:

Boys and Girls in all three categories:

- sex (male or female, as appropriate)
- age (15–18)
- social class (working class)
- race (white)

Assaultive Offenders:

- contact physical violence (assault)
- age of victim (14–50)
- sex of victim (male or female)
- victim relationship (stranger, relative, or acquaintance)

Sexual Offenders:

- contact sexual violence (fondling to penetration)
- age of at least one victim (14 or younger)
- sex of victims (male or female)
- victim relationship (stranger, relative, or acquaintance)

Finally, the life-history method is particularly relevant because it richly documents personal reflexive deliberations, choices, experiences, and transformations over time. A life history records "the relation between the social conditions that determine practice and the future social world that practice brings into being" (Connell 1995: 89). The life-history method is what William I. Thomas and Florian Znaniecki (1927) characterized as the "perfect" type of sociological material. Such classics of criminology as Clifford Shaw's (1930) *The Jack Roller*, Edwin Sutherland's (1937) *The Professional Thief*, and William Chambliss's (1972) *The Box Man* illustrate the "power of life-history data to illuminate the complex processes of criminal offending" (Sampson and Laub 1993: 203). Indeed, the life-history method recently experienced a resurgence in the social sciences, and the resurgence is due in part to the fact that life histories tap continuous "lived experiences" of individuals. That is, the method demands a close evaluation of the meaning of social life for those who enact it—revealing their reflexive deliberations, choices, experiences, embodied practices, and social world. As Terri Orbuch (1997: 455) points out in her important article "People's Accounts Count," the life history is significant sociologically because we gain "insight into human experience and arrive at meanings or culturally embedded normative explanations," insight that allows us to understand "the ways in which people organize views of themselves, of others, and of their social world." And Ken Plummer (2001: 242) eloquently summarized the value of life histories:

To tell the story of a life may be at the heart of our cultures: connecting the inner world to the outer world, speaking to the subjective and the objective, establishing the boundaries of identities (of who one is and who one is not); crossing "brute being"—embodied and emotional—with "knowing self"— rational and irrational; making links across life phases and cohort generations; revealing historical shifts in a culture; establishing collective memories and imagined communities; telling of the concerns of their time and place.

Although individuals engage in violent and nonviolent embodied practices, this does not mean that everything about a person is accessible immediately to that person as well as to others—there is mystery. Yet the social process of becoming violent or nonviolent can be decoded by a reconstruction of the life history that relates later events to earlier reflexive deliberations, choices, interactions, and practices (Connell 1987). Such life-history accounts are "destined to bring to light" the embodied practices by which an individual makes himself or herself a person (Sartre 1956: 734). As Robert Agnew (1990: 271) points out, these types of accounts of those involved in crime "may be the only way of obtaining accurate information on the individual's internal states and those aspects of the external situation that the individual is attending to."

In addition to in-depth documentation of an individual's social world and representations of reflexive deliberation, choice, interaction, and embodied practice, the life history links the social and historical context in which both are embedded. As Raewyn Connell (1995: 89) points out, "The project that is documented in a life-history story is itself the relation between the social conditions that determine practice and the future social world that practice brings into being. That is to say, life-history method always concerns the making of social life through time. It is literally history."

Thus one salient feature of the life-history method in exploring assaultive and sexual violence by boys and girls is that it permits an in-depth understanding of the interplay between social structures and personal experience. The life history can reveal what other methods can hide or obscure. The research here embraces a theorized life history as the specific method because the interviewing and interpretation are based on structured action theory (Connell 1991; Dowsett 1996). This particular procedure is "not a process of theorization by generalization, but a systematic method of investigating the operation of social processes through the recounted experiences of individual lives" (Dowsett 1996: 50).[2]

Sample

Life-history research does not target large and representative samples from which to draw bold generalizations. Rather, in this study its goal is to uncover patterns and to provide useful cases that signal contributing factors to assaultive and sexual violence and nonviolence by white working-class adolescent boys and girls. Indeed, the sampling procedure can be best described as "stratified purposeful sampling" (Patton 1990: 172–74) to fit the theorized life-history method.

First, twenty white working-class adolescent boys and girls currently incarcerated, on probation, or undergoing private counseling for assaultive or sexual violence were selected to match the demographic variables identified earlier and then were categorized as "assaultive offender" (five boys and five girls) and "sexual offender" (five boys and five girls). I chose these adolescents to avoid limiting the sample to boys and girls officially processed in the juvenile justice system. The incarcerated and on-probation boys and girls were identified by prison personnel or juvenile probation officers, who obtained the informed consent of each youth and their parents or guardians before I interviewed them. In private counseling, the boys and girls were identified similarly by therapists prior to informed-consent interviews with me.

Second, ten white working-class adolescent boys and girls who denied committing, and had not been formally charged with committing, a sexually violent and/or assaultive offense (or admitted committing an assaultive act in the past but for a very short period of time) were selected (according to relevant demographic variables) with the assistance of representatives from the Boys and Girls Clubs and the use of a "snowballing" approach and were categorized as "nonviolent boys and girls."

Sampling continued until no new relevant themes or patterns emerged: during the interviews, "data saturation" occurred as soon as specific themes and patterns appeared with regularity.

Additionally, I obtained a "mix" of youth from different family configurations (e.g., adoptive parents versus biological parents; violent versus nonviolent homes), yet all the youth reported in this particular book grew up in *nonviolent* households; that is, they did not engage in violence against family members nor were they the victims of assaultive or sexual violence by family members. Despite this nonviolent home life, the "maximum-variation" sampling procedure provided a selection of boys and girls from a wide range of family relations and other background situations. The vast majority of the boys and girls simultaneously grew up in the same milieu (lived in the same neighborhood and attended the same school). The race and social class of the entire sample remained constant (white working class).

Some argue that we learn little from such a small sample. However, a detailed investigation of a few case studies often illuminates contributing factors concealed by other methodologies. Gary Dowsett (1996) points out that in other disciplines, such as the medical community, scholars frequently publish research based on a limited number of clinically observed cases. For example, a 1990 article published in the *American Journal of Public Health* documented:

> HIV seroconversions in gay men, related, it seems, exclusively to receptive oral intercourse with swallowed ejaculate. Given the ongoing unresolved debate about the likelihood of HIV transmission through oral-genital sex, this was a sensational finding. The article, however, was based on two cases, and although the authors' conclusions were properly cautionary, the example demonstrates that the chief concern need not always be the sampling method and sample size. (Dowsett 1996: 44)

Nevertheless, thirty case studies is not a representative sample and, therefore, my conclusions—although properly cautionary—are illustrative and suggestive only. Notwithstanding the article just cited, the six life stories reported in chapters 3, 4, and 5 (three boys and three girls) simultaneously show that important aspects of assaultive and sexual violence and nonviolence by white working-class teenagers have been overlooked and, therefore, present an extremely rich source for further investigation and theory building. As Solomin Kobrin (1982: 153) pointed out thirty years ago, life histories reveal the more "elusive elements of deviant behavior that are often difficult to capture in quantifiable variables." Each life story deepens and augments our understanding of the situational accomplishment of gender and sexuality and of the eventual use of assaultive violence, sexual violence, or nonviolence as a result of personal life history.

Data Collection

The theorized life-history method implemented here involved voluntary and confidential one-on-one tape-recorded "informal conversational interviews" (Patton 1990: 280–82). These conversations were conducted in private, secluded rooms and were completed in two meetings of three hours each. The conversations were fluid, allowing each boy and girl to take the lead rather than merely to respond to topical questions. The goal was to grasp each individual's unique viewpoint—his or her personal vision of the world. This interview method involved attempting to foster collaboration (rather than hierarchy) in the research process by judiciously engaging each boy and girl, "working interactionally to establish the discursive bases from which the respondent can articulate his or her relevant experiences" (Holstein and Gubrium 1995: 47). I used an "open coding" methodology, or line-by-line examination of each life history to identify recurrent themes and patterns (see Strauss and Corbin 1998).

This does not mean, however, that the conversations were unstructured. On the contrary, each conversation attempted to unearth the reflexive deliberations and choices made, the situational interactions and accomplishment of embodied gender and sexual practices, and the eventual use of violence and nonviolence in particular contexts and as a result of personal life history. As such, the interviews drew on the insights of structured action theory. I specifically sought detailed descriptions of reflexive deliberations, choices, and practices (what a boy or girl did and why they chose to do it) and accounts of interaction in families, peer and leisure groups, and schools. The conversations touched on intimate and sensitive areas of personal life and relationships. Topical examples I explored include (1) the division of labor between men and women in the adolescent's household and in the peer and leisure groups of which he or she is a member; (2) the power dynamics between male and female adults, between adults and children, among boys, among girls, and between boys and girls at school and in peer groups; (3) any masculine or feminine mentoring during childhood and adolescence and "moment of engagement"; (4) his or her sexual awakening and "moment of engagement," how he or she managed it, and how images of sexuality were conveyed to him or her and related to gender; (5) the meaning and practices of embodied gender and sexual behavior and violence throughout his or her life course and how they were represented to him or her; (6) the tensions and conflicts in these processes and the way they changed over time; and (7) all gender and sexual challenges and violent events during each life course.

Limitations of the Study

Although life-history research provides rich areas of criminological knowledge, it is not without limitation. Indeed, there are traditional problems related to investigator effects; for example, the investigator recounts only part of the story. However, as James Short responds, this criticism should not be seen as unique to life-history data: "Different methods tell different parts of a story and tell them differently" (1982: 135). As we know, all knowledge is partial and situated, derived in part from the researcher's authority and privilege (Richardson 1990). Life stories must be seen as active constructs in themselves, jointly developed by interviewer and interviewee (Presser 2008). In critically assessing my place and position during each conversation, I followed suggestions of feminist sociologists that interviewers attempt to give up "authority over the people we study, but not the responsibility of authorship of our texts" (Reinhartz 1992: 28). This involved developing strategies to empower the interviewees during our interaction. For example, I met each adolescent twice, using the second conversation to carefully review together the content of the earlier conversation. This helped to break down hierarchy, to encourage the interviewees to find and speak the "correctness" of their stories, and to avoid treating each participant simply as an object of study.

Moreover, although all interviews are gendered contexts— whether they are single or mixed gender (this study involves both)—research suggests that the sex of "the interviewer is not an insurmountable barrier to establishing rapport and achieving reliable results in in-depth interviewing" (Williams and Heikes 1993: 289–90). Being especially concerned about interviewing across sex, gender, class, and age (i.e., an adult middle-class man interviewing working-class teenage girls), I was encouraged to find that some studies comparing male and female researchers have established that the "definitions of the situation" conveyed by respondents (regardless of interviewer sex and gender) show "remarkable similarity and overlap, even on topics involving gender and sexuality, which have been identified by survey researchers as the topics most sensitive to 'sex of interviewer effects'" (Williams and Heikes 1993: 289). Importantly, however, such a result is reached only by the researcher acknowledging from the outset that sex and gender are inevitable aspects of the research setting and by taking into account this inevitability in their research practice (Padfield and Procter 1996). Consequently, from the beginning of the research process I took steps to decrease sex and gender as salient issues during each interview. For example, I asked those obtaining the necessary informed consent (prison personnel, probation officers, and therapists) to ask each potential respondent if he or she had a "problem" talking with an adult man about intimate and possibly painful life experiences—not one boy or girl declined participation. Moreover, throughout our conversations I attempted to be mindful of sex and gender construction and worked at minimizing hierarchy and maximizing collaboration and reciprocity. Following the suggestions of Margaret Andersen (1993) for "researching across difference," I did not present myself as an expert; I did not assume the passivity of respondents; and I did not force respondents to adapt to my definition of the interview situation. Rather, I emphasized how sincerely interested I was in learning about their lives from their points of view—I respected these adolescents as experts of their own life histories; I discussed with each interviewee selected aspects of my own life (including my experiences with violent victimization); and I enthusiastically answered any questions they posed to me. Moreover, I did not hide any emotions that developed out of heartrending accounts of certain events in their life stories. And my efforts seemed to have worked. At the end of the first interview respondents were asked if they would agree to a follow-up conversation—all but two boys agreed to a second interview, most with enthusiasm.[3] Additionally, the vast majority expressed excitement that I might include their life story in "a book." Overall, I believe that both the boys and the girls were trusting, open, and could have talked with me for many more hours than we shared. Although the adolescents I interviewed may report different things to a female interviewer, this does not make the life stories reported here any less salient and "honest." As Andersen points out: "If the task of sociology is to understand the multiple interactions between social structure and biographies, then the many ways in which we see ourselves and our relationships to others should be part of sociological accounts" (1993: 51).

The possibilities that respondents may, for example, lack memory of key events and/or issues or simply attempt to deceive the interviewer is an additional cautionary concern in life-history methodology. However, I agree with Robert Agnew's argument that there is no a priori reason to assume that boys and girls are more likely to be dishonest or subject to faulty memory during, for example, life-history interviews than they are when participating in such other procedures as self-report questionnaires and large-scale surveys. In each of these methodologies, answers to questions reflect the "respondents' perception of reality and events" (Agnew 1990: 269). Given that such "contaminants" may occur in any social science methodology, I chose to examine carefully what is expressed in each conversation and to treat each life history as a *situational truth*. As Ann Goetting (1999: 20) points out, life stories are not simply "true" representations of an objective "reality"; rather, the interpretations of both interviewer and interviewee "combine to create a particular view of reality" (see further, Presser 2008).

Of necessity, I have built in research strategies that increase the credibility of findings. Prior to commencing an interview in a secluded room, I explained that risk of identification was negligible inasmuch as all interview information would be identified by a number only, stored in a secure facility, and destroyed by me at the conclusion of the study. Moreover, I pointed out that interview conversations would be treated with strict confidence, never made available to another person or agency, and that certain identifying details would be changed. Further, I obtained an informed consent prior to each interview. I also indicated that the final results of the research would be published in a manner that fully protects the anonymity of the interviewees, family members, and all others mentioned during the interview. In addition, I addressed topics in different ways and at varying times during the interview. Interestingly, the answers rarely varied. Importantly, not only did I point out that our conversations would address issues that might be painful and stressful, I emphatically emphasized to each interviewee that they did not have to answer a question or talk about an issue if they chose not to. I consistently revisited the consent issue during our conversations, and underscored to each that he or she could stop taking part in the study at any time, for any reason.

Finally, in addition to joint construct, boys' and girls' accounts, like all interview data, probably are affected by meanings that are external to the conversation—such as what boys and girls learned in treatment and/or incarceration. Therefore, I specifically discussed with each respondent whether his or her responses were shaped by such experiences; that is, was his or her past behavior reinterpreted during our conversations, in light of personal experiences in treatment, during incarceration, or while on probation. I consistently asked each respondent to recapture the past and respond as to how he or she conceptualized choices and events at the time of enactment; that is, I probed their reflexivity and internal deliberations. In all cases, the boys and girls seemed able to distinguish between what they learned in treatment and/or during incarceration about their behavior and what they internally deliberated about in the past when the particular event occurred. Moreover, I discussed with therapists, counselors, and probation officers the nature of any treatment received by each boy and girl. For all participants in this study, gender and sexuality were never a remedial part of their rehabilitation.

Although it is critical to verify factual information and consistency in storytelling, the primary task of the life-history researcher is not to establish an alleged "truth" but to describe—as stated earlier—how each particular life story assembles a specific situational truth. What is most critical is that the life story is "true" for the interviewee at that moment—that it captures an individual's personal reality and his or her unique definition of the situation. The aim is not simply to relate a particular life history to other cases in the project and to previous research findings (which I do), but to grasp each story for what it tells us about that specific case. In short, each conversation attempted to comprehend the revealed reflexive choices and embodied practices made during the respondent's life course, the formation of gender and sexual practices, and the use of assaultive or sexual violence or nonviolence as outcomes of a personal trajectory constrained by his or her social structural position.

Data Analysis

Aware that there is "no such thing as an authentic experience unmediated by interpretation" and that "reaching conclusions in research is a social process and interpretation of data is always a 'political, contested and unstable activity'" (Burman, Batchelor, and Brown 2001: 454), my data analysis had two stages. First, tape-recorded conversations were transcribed and thoroughly analyzed, and individual case studies were prepared. Second, the life histories were dissected to define similarities and differences among the pathways to assaultive violence, sexual violence, and nonviolence. Consistent with other theorized life-history methodology, the intent here is not simply to present biography but to explain social process through the life-history data (Connell 1995; Dowsett 1996).

The chapters that follow attempt to capture each interviewee's embodied experience in his or her words. As such, I examine how individual social interaction with others is embedded in social structural constraints and reflexivity in particular settings. Moreover, by comparing individual life stories we can establish links among boys and among girls whose lives are quite different but who are affected by similar race and class position as well as growing up in a nonviolent household. In other words, we can discover the interconnections among boys and girls—as well as the differences and similarities between them—who live in a shared social context. Accordingly, theorized life-history methodology helps to register patterns in lives that other methodologies render invisible. And, as shown throughout chapters 3, 4, and 5, there is much here to offer in our attempt to understand youth assaultive violence, sexual violence, and nonviolence.

Bullying as a Gender and Sexual Challenge

All of the six youth discussed in this book were serious victims of bullying at school. Bullying among youth is a serious social problem, and remains endemic among secondary-school students in the United States. For example, approximately 30 percent of twelve- to eighteen-year-old students report having been bullied at school during the previous six months (National Center for Education Statistics 2008). Of these students, 53 percent report having been bullied once or twice during that period, 25 percent once or twice a month, 11 percent once or twice a week, and 8 percent daily (3). I define *bully* as one who unilaterally engages in harmful, offensive, and/or intimidating conduct against another who is physically, mentally, and/or socially weaker than s/he. In other words, bullying is one example of a gender and sexual challenge referred to earlier.

There exist three major types of bullying in secondary schools: *verbal* (name-calling, humiliation, mocking, insulting), *social* (exclusion from peer groups, gossiping, rumor-mongering), and *physical* (hitting, shoving, kicking, beating up). Despite adolescent girls' and boys' involvement in all three forms of bullying, and the fact that boys bully more than girls and boys are victimized more often than girls (Meyer 2009), studies suggest that girls engage principally in verbal and social forms of bullying while boys predominate in physical forms of bullying (Pronk and Zimmer-Gembeck 2010; Reynolds and Repetti 2010). Studies across North America and Europe reveal that the two most common reasons students are bullied at school are "bodily appearance" (perceived by others as skinny or obese and/or displaying a gender/sexuality nonnormative presentation) and "bodily practice" (perceived by others as acting in a shy, insecure, and/ or gender/sexuality nonnormative manner) (Erling and Hwang 2004; Perry, Hodges, and Egan 2001; Rigby 2002; Sweeting and West 2001). Indeed, the most frequent responses in a study of 119 secondary-school students in the United States that asked "Who gets bullied?" reported 40 percent answered because of their bodily appearance and 36 percent because of their bodily practice; a more recent study of close to twelve thousand secondary students representing twenty-five schools in twelve states found that 55 percent of bullying incidents focused on "looks" and 37 percent on "body shape" (Davis and Nixon 2010; Frisen, Jonsson, and Persson 2007; and see further, Lumeng et al. 2010). Moreover, this emphasis on the body varies by sex, girls reporting a slightly greater amount for "looks" (58 percent of girls as opposed to 50 percent of boys are bullied) and for "body shape" (40 percent of girls in contrast with 30 percent of boys are bullied) (Davis and Nixon 2010).

In addition to the importance of the body to bullying (and in particular its gender/sexual nonnormative aspects), being bullied has been found to be strongly associated with *reactive* bullying and violence by those frequently victimized. For example, a predominant pattern in school shootings (by students) is that nearly all of the "school shooters" since the 1990s (at both secondary-school and college levels) had themselves been bullied consistently at school. What the case studies of school shooters and other research reveal, then, is that bullying in school often has devastating effects on the initial victims of bullying and may lead to such victims engaging in severe forms of interpersonal violence at school (Klein 2011). Yet, the school-shooting cases signal not only the close association between being bullied and reactive in-school violent behavior, but also beg at least two salient questions: Why the relationship between being bullied and reactive *in-school* violence? And is there a similar relationship between being bullied in school and reactive *outside-school* violence?

Although there is increasing interest in why individuals who themselves are bullied engage in reactive in-school violence (Kimmel and Mahler 2003; Klein 2011), no research has yet examined the actual "microlevel" in-school embodied gendered and sexual social processes and dynamics leading from having been bullied to engaging specifically in assaultive and sexual offenses either outside or inside school by adolescent boys and girls—that is, how embodied interaction in a particular local in-school gendered and sexual milieu may be related to engaging in assaultive and sexual offenses by teenage boys and girls inside or outside school boundaries. Not surprisingly, examination of the relationship among prior bullying victimization, the body, sex, gender, sexuality, and subsequent engagement in outside- and in-school violence, remains a pressing and crucial area of study. This book seeks to remedy these crucial oversights by scrutinizing the movement from having been bullied to engaging specifically in reactive inside- as well as outside-school assaultive and sexual offenses, and how this reactive social process is related specifically to embodied sex, gender, and sexuality by adolescent boys and girls.

During the interviews in this study, *all* of the boys and girls consistently expressed a deep concern about the role of "the body" in their everyday life, its relation to sex, gender, and sexual interaction, and ultimately, its relation to in-school bullying and inside/outside-school assaultive and sexual violence. Interestingly, initially I did not plan to include "the body" as a topic of conversation—it was not part of the prepared interview schedule—yet each of the interviewees intensely expressed its importance in her/his daily life. In other words, the body was a salient saturated *theme* throughout the data. A saturated *pattern*

of moving from having been bullied to engaging in reactive assaultive and sexual offending involves three stages—what I call
(1) repression, (2) reflexivity, and (3) recognition—each of which
is related to the body, sex, gender, and sexuality. In what follows
in chapters 3, 4, and 5, I illustrate how the above theme (the
body) and pattern (the three-stage social process) are related to
the struggle for gender and sexual recognition through a discussion of six of the individual case studies.

3

Assaultive Violence

Lenny and Kelly

Chapter 3 focuses on a white working-class boy and girl involved in assaultive violence: Lenny and Kelly (both pseudonyms). Lenny and Kelly were chosen from the larger pool of interviewees for three explicit reasons. First, neither personally experienced physical or sexual violence in their childhood home. Thus, these two case studies facilitate comparison as to why a boy and a girl may eventually engage in assaultive violence despite growing up in a home setting in which they were not physically or sexually victimized. Second, Lenny (male sex category) and Kelly (female sex category) represent differently constructed masculinities—"wimp" (Lenny) and "bully" (Kelly)—and therefore typify two significantly contrasting sexed and gendered pathways into assaultive violence at school and on the street. Finally, these two case studies are nicely juxtaposed because both Lenny and Kelly grew up in the same neighborhood and attended the same school at the same time. Accordingly, this chapter reports data as to why a boy and a girl from the *same* social milieu engage in assaultive violence for different reasons yet in the same school and street settings. We begin this chapter with Lenny.

Lenny

Lenny was a short, obese, and somewhat shy fifteen-year-old. He had short dark hair and wore blue jeans, a sweatshirt, and tennis shoes to each interview. He also wore a cap that was emblazoned "Give Blood, Play Hockey," yet he spoke to me in a skittish and soft-spoken manner. Although never formally charged or arrested for assaultive violence, at the time of the interviews Lenny was attending private counseling sessions for continually assaulting younger and smaller neighborhood boys. In what follows, I describe, through Lenny's words, his family relations at home and assaultive violence at school and on the street.

Family Relations

Lenny lived in a working-class neighborhood with his mother and father, an older brother (aged eighteen), and a younger sister (aged thirteen). The family lived in a two-bedroom upstairs apartment. Lenny had another brother (aged twenty-one) who did not live with the family. Lenny's earliest family memory is of the first time the family went camping: "We had a great time together, right by a lake, canoeing, hiking, roasting marshmallows and stuff."

Although both parents worked outside the home as unskilled laborers, the mother and sister were responsible for all domestic labor (the father did no domestic labor); they received only limited help from Lenny and his brother. Lenny and his brother shared a room; all three children were responsible for cleaning their respective rooms. This was not a problem because Lenny and his brother alternated cleaning the room they shared, and there seemed to be little quarrel regarding this. Lenny also reported a very warm and affectionate family environment: "My parents have a kinda family thing. We do things together. We go to beaches, camping, have cookouts, go to the movies. A lot of things I guess." However, Lenny mostly liked to do things with his father. Asked about his favorite activities, Lenny replied, "We go hunting each year—my father, my brothers, and me.

My father bought me a 30/30. And I got my hunting license. My father helped me study to get my license. I studied with him. That was fun."

Asked further about hunting, Lenny said: "It's exciting to get ready 'cause we eat a big supper before and get up early and go. It's fun to be with my dad." I inquired about other activities Lenny did with his father, and he emphasized fishing, swimming, playing catch, and playing darts. "The whole family, we play board games; that's real fun."

Lenny's mother never disciplined Lenny and the other children. The father "took control" when he came home from work: "He never actually hit me, he just would get mad and talk serious to me. We didn't make him mad that much. We'd do what my dad and mom says."

At home, then, Lenny grew up under a conventional gender division of labor. Both parents performed "appropriate" gendered labor and other home-related activities—his father embodied a localized hegemonic masculinity in relation to his mother's emphasized femininity. Although Lenny's father was never physically violent, clearly he held the power in the family and used that power to control all decisions. For example, even when Lenny wanted to do something outside the home (e.g., go bike riding), he was not allowed to do it unless his father approved ahead of time. Lenny identified with his father—his initial model for developing an embodied conception of masculinity—engaging in accountably localized masculine appearance and practices (e.g., hunting, fishing, playing catch, etc.). Lenny thrived on his father's approval, such as when he shot his first deer ("Dad said he was real proud of me"), and conceptualized maleness as, in part, embracing the embodied practices of "working hard, being strong, a good hunter, and being like Dad." It was at home then where Lenny initially took up a project of masculinity as his own. And given Lenny's success at constructing such masculine appearance and practices—his fundamental gender project was to be "like Dad"—he never was the victim of nor did he ever engage in assaultive/sexual violence in the home milieu. Thus, although Lenny's father maintained a hegemonic masculine relation to Lenny's mother's emphasized femininity, between father and son a superior/inferior hierarchical relationship existed, involving a dominating masculine father and an accountably subordinate masculine son.

School, Street, and Assaultive Violence

Lenny did reasonably well in elementary and junior high school. For the most part he liked his teachers and the schools, and he earned average grades. Most recently, in eighth grade, he graduated with honors. For that, he got a new bike: "All my uncles and aunts, my mom and dad, they all pitched in and bought me a[n] eighteen-speed. Pretty cool."

Nevertheless, at school Lenny received constant verbal bullying because of his physical size and shape (shorter and heavier than the other boys and girls). Other children—especially the dominant popular boys—call him a "slob," a "fat pig," a "wimp," and a "punk," and thus a hegemonic-subordinate relationship was established in school between the popular boys (hegemonic) and Lenny (subordinate). Moreover, at school kids continually bullied him about his mother, whom they saw as extremely obese: "Kids always say my mom is so fat, you know, and things like that. Kids say that my mom is so stupid. They call her all kinds of names, and some swear words—like she has a[n] elephant ass." Because of this verbal bullying, Lenny developed a dislike of school: "I hated to go to school." When asked if he discussed this abuse with his mother and father, Lenny replied: "My dad said that if somebody punches me, then I get the right to punch him back. If I'm being teased, I tease him right back. Call him names back. If they [sic] teasing me always, then my dad tells me that I should punch 'em back."

Lenny reflexively deliberated feeling embarrassed at school because of his physical size and shape, and because of his obese mother. Moreover, because he was smaller than the kids abusing him, he felt insecure about responding as his father taught him. He stated that the people abusing him were the dominant "tough guys" in the school: "They was the popular tough guys, and everyone laughed when I didn't do nothin'. I couldn't. I felt really small in front of everybody."

Consequently, because of his embodied subordinate masculinity at school, Lenny became a loner and decided he must attempt to avoid the masculine dominant "tough guys." In addition, Lenny observed that other kids in school were being abused: some "would do nothin', like me, and some would fight." It seems there were many school fights based on verbal bullying. Lenny recalled the following example: "One time I was sitting down by my locker and the big guys teased this kid. He [the bullied boy] hit the kid back, and he [the big guy] had a lot of friends, and they all jumped in on that one kid." These types of events, then, led Lenny reflexively to become frightened of social interaction at school; accordingly, he decided to avoid school as much as possible. Indeed, there were fights in Lenny's school "about once every month"; apparently kids would fight about "everything." Lenny provided another example:

Like one time a kid stole the other kid's comic cards. When he was in the hallway with them, the other kid came over and the kid gave 'em back but he beat him up 'cause he took 'em, over that. The kid gave 'em back to him, but he still beat him up. So I was always scared to talk to kids. I'd never know what might happen. So I went to school, went to my classes, and then ran home.

Q. Are these tough kids looked up to in your school?

A. Oh yeah. They are the neat kids. Everybody wanted to be tough like them.

Q. You wanted to be tough like them, too?

A. Yeah, I wanted to be like them.

Lenny determined that he wanted to be like the dominant "tough guys" at school; he longed to go home and tell his father that he did not let anyone push him around at school. However, he was unable to embody dominant masculinity as interaction with his father (and at school) had emphasized—which terrified him: "I couldn't tell my dad that I was afraid, 'cause then even him would call me a wimp, a scaredy-cat." By the time Lenny was fourteen, then, he lacked masculine bodily resources and thus reflexively felt extremely inferior at school—he "failed" to embody dominant masculinity in this setting. Nevertheless, one school event provided an opportunity for Lenny to attempt masculinity as practiced by the boys who bullied him:

Q. Tell me about that.

A. There was this nerd of a kid that even I made fun of. He would wear high-waters.

Q. What are high-waters?

A. Kids that wear high pants.

Q. Okay, go on.

A. This high-water is real skinny and ugly. I'm bigger than him. So I go: "You look funny in those pants," and stuff like that. I called him a nerd and he said the same back to me. There was all these kids around, and so I beat him up in the hallway 'cause he called me a nerd and nobody liked him.

Q. Why did you hit him?

A. 'Cause he called me a name that I didn't like and I wasn't afraid of him.

Q. What did other kids say who saw you beat him up?

A. Some kids was happy 'cause nobody likes him. But some said I should pick on kids my own size. Plus I got ISS [in-school suspension].

Q. Did you tell your dad about this fight?

A. Yeah. I ran home and told him that this kid was making fun of me, so I beat him up and got ISS for it.

Q. Did your father talk to the school officials about the fight?

A. Nope. He was just happy I beat up the kid.

Q. Is that the only fight in school?

A. Yeah, 'cause he is the kid I can beat up at school. I can beat up kids in my neighborhood.

Lenny indicated that the assault of the "high-water" was his only school fight. He then provided detailed information about his involvement in neighborhood violence, the setting where his assaultive behavior concentrated. According to Lenny, numerous neighborhood boys would constantly challenge him to physical fights. However, he reflexively developed specific criteria for his participation in such challenges: "I fight if I can beat the kid. I got this kid next door, he calls me a fag. I mean, there is no reason why he calls me a fag, and my father said next time he does that, 'beat him up.' My father says if I don't fight him, he'll [father] fight me. So I beat the kid up, and my father was happy."

Q. Was this kid smaller than you?

A. Oh yeah; I only fight kids I can beat up. My father says that's smart; you should only "pick the battles you can win."

Q. How did it make you feel when you beat up neighborhood kids?

A. It made me feel real good inside. I knew I wasn't a wimp anymore.

Q. Did it bother you that the boys you beat up were smaller than you?

A. No, 'cause of what my dad said. And I fought kids that called me names or said stuff about Mom.

Q. Who are your friends?

A. I don't have friends at school. Only kids in my neighborhood. I play with kids that are younger than me. We have fun together.

Thus, in the "site" of his neighborhood street, Lenny embodied a dominating form of masculinity in relation to the subordinate masculinities of the smaller and younger boys, as he was now "calling the shots" and "running the show."

I discussed sexuality with Lenny. He told me he did not learn about sex from his parents but from "sex-ed" class at school. He also heard kids talking about sex with each other at school: "Some kids, even fourteen- and fifteen-year-olds, you know, are having sex in my school. And they talk about it, right out loud." Lenny never had a girlfriend or went on a date.

However, occasionally he attended school dances and danced with several girls, but nothing ever developed. After the dance "I'd just go home." He asked girls for dates numerous times, but all refused. This bothered him somewhat because he wanted a girlfriend with whom to experience sexuality and to have someone close with whom he could talk. It was at this time then that Lenny began to affix a heterosexual project to his masculinity. However, his conception of heterosexuality is that it need not be relentless or incessant:

> Q. Did you ever feel you should have sex with girls?
>
> A. No.
>
> Q. Other kids were bragging about having sex, and did that make you feel you should also have sex to be cool?
>
> A. No, never. You don't have to have sex to be cool.

Lenny perceived himself as heterosexual, without feeling that he had to "go out there and do it." If he had a girlfriend, he reasoned that he would like to experience sexuality because he was still a "virgin." However, Lenny pointed out that it did not bother him that he had not experienced sex: "It'll come someday." Although the dominant "cool guys" were also the boys who publicly bragged about "getting laid," Lenny reflexively decided there existed numerous avenues to "being cool": "Some kids are cool because of the clothes they're wearing. Some kids smoke. Some are tough. Some play sports, rollerblading, biking. Not all cool kids have sex."

Lenny added that there were five major boy cliques in his school—the "jocks" (the tough and cool guys) who represented dominant/dominating (and occasionally) hegemonic masculinity, the "nerds," the "smart kids," the "wimps," and the "losers," as various forms of subordinate masculinities. It is the relationship between such masculinities that constructs an informal boy clique social structure in Lenny's school. Lenny reflexively decided that some of the dominant jocks most likely considered him a nerd and a wimp because they always verbally bullied him—not only for his size and shape but also because he did not "fight back" and did not participate in any sport: "The jocks always teased the nerds and make fun of them for not playing sports." According to the jocks, those (including Lenny) who did not play sports (especially football) and who did not retaliate in kind when bullied were subordinated as "wimps" and "nerds," thus (as stated earlier) constructing a momentary hegemonic masculinity. In fact, Lenny stated that jocks often called him a wimp because he did not play football and because he was not tough: "The jocks called me a wimp because they said I was afraid of gettin' tackled and afraid of fighting." It was this verbal bullying that constructed a gender challenge for Lenny, as he embodied a subordinate masculinity within the school setting.

Q. Did you feel you were a wimp and a nerd?

A. Yeah, I did. I wanted to be tough like them, and I was tough to some kids.

Q. How did it make you feel when you were tough with some kids?

A. I didn't feel like I was a wimp anymore. I felt good. My dad said there's always someone bigger. And that goes for the big kids too. There are people who can beat them up.

Q. What does it mean, then, to be a "real man"?

A. To be tough, have muscles. Just big like my father, he's about six feet something. A good fighter like the guys at school.

Q. Do you want to be a "real man"?

A. Yeah! I want to get muscles because I want to be kinda strong in case people fight me. I want to be able to get them down, not to hurt them, but to get them down so they don't hurt me. I don't want them to fight me. I want to be strong enough to get them down.

I asked Lenny if there was anything else that he would include in his definition of a "real man." Surprisingly, he stated the following: "A real man is also a gentleman. That's a man. A man that don't hit girls. A man that hits girls is not a man."

Q. Where did you learn that?

A. From my father. My sister used to hit me, and I got really mad at her. I'd say, "I'm gonna punch you if you don't stop it." And my father says, "I don't think so." I threaten to punch her but my father says, "I don't think so."

Q. Your father taught you not to hit girls?

A. Yeah. He says boys should never hit girls. It's okay to hit boys but not girls. That's what he taught me.

Q. Did your father ever hit your mother?

A. Never.

When I asked Lenny whether there were gay and lesbian kids in his school, he stated that he did not know of any, but: "There is a gay person in my family. My brother, he's gay." Lenny's older brother (the twenty-one-year-old) is gay; his brother's sexual orientation seemed to be accepted by Lenny's family: "Yeah, my family don't care. He comes over to my house. My family likes him. We had a cookout with him and his boyfriend. We all had a great time."

Q. So you know the difference between heterosexuality and homosexuality?

A. Of course.

Q. Should you be heterosexual to be a "real man"?

A. What? My brother is a real man. He's tall like my father and he lifts weights in his basement, so he's strong. He bikes and jogs and stuff. And he could fight if he wanted.

Kelly

Kelly is a short, stocky, seventeen-year-old who eloquently presented her life history. At each interview she met me without makeup, with her shoulder-length blonde hair always pulled back in a ponytail, and wearing the same worker boots, baggy jeans, and sweatshirt with a hood. Kelly currently is on probation for an assault conviction. In what follows, I describe, through Kelly's words, her family relations at home and assaultive violence at school and on the street.

Family Relations

Kelly's earliest childhood memory is when her youngest sister was born; Kelly was three at the time. The birth impacted her because she was no longer "the baby" of the family and no longer received the attention she had in the past. Nevertheless, Kelly's mother comforted her by stating that having three daughters was like having cookies and cream: "I was the cream and my two sisters were the cookies." That is the last "nice thing" Kelly remembers her mother ever saying to her.

Kelly lived with her biological mother, a stepfather (she never met her biological father), a younger sister (by three years), and an older sister (by four years). Her stepfather was a factory worker and her mother "just stayed at home." When I asked Kelly if her mother was a homemaker, she responded: "Yeah, if that's what you call it. A drunken homemaker!" Although Kelly's mother occasionally would clean the house, do some laundry, and cook a few family meals, she spent most of her daily hours "drinking alcohol and watching TV." The only household labor Kelly's stepfather did was taking the trash to the town dump, building household furniture, and "keeping his cars and snowmobiles running." As such, Kelly grew up among an explicit gender division of household labor. In addition, Kelly's stepfather was physically violent and verbally abusive to Kelly's mother. As Kelly put it:

> My stepfather would come home from work, like every night, and start to yell and beat on my mom. She was always drunk and hardly did what he wanted, like clean and have dinner ready. So he would yell at her for that, you know, and she'd try to block him but she couldn't. She was too weak. He'd hit her, punch her, kick her, throw her all over the house.

Thus Kelly grew up confronting patriarchal relations at home, in which the stepfather frequently wielded power through physical and verbal abuse over the mother—the stepfather embodied localized hegemonic masculinity and the mother emphasized femininity.

The family never did anything together "as a whole family," as it was divided profoundly between mother and sisters on the one side and Kelly and her stepfather on the other side. Because her mother was either occupied with her younger sister or "too drunk" to interact with her (and her older sister was away from home "as much as possible"), Kelly reflexively decided to spend most of her time with her stepfather. Kelly chose to turn to her stepfather for warmth and affection, and considered him to be her primary parent because they did "everything" together: "We played around with cars, played games, built furniture and stuff, and worked on his cars and snowmobile." Kelly's stepfather ignored all other members of the family—except when physically and verbally abusing them—yet engaged in "quality time" with Kelly: "He would tuck me in at night. He would let me sit on his lap when we watched TV. He'd give me hugs and kisses good night. He'd carry me on his shoulders. He'd give me piggyback rides. And he'd twirl me around with my hands. And I was the only one who got to go riding the snowmobile with him. He basically ignored my sisters."

Although he practiced a violent and physically powerful hegemonic masculinity, Kelly became extremely attached to her stepfather. This mutual affection and devotion between Kelly and her stepfather provided an escape from her overtly oppressive home environment: Kelly reflexively adopted what her stepfather practiced. That is, Kelly decided to appropriate his type of masculinity as her own, rather than the femininity of her mother or her older sister, and thus it was in this setting where Kelly first took up a project of masculinity. Consider the following response when I asked Kelly what she learned from her stepfather: "He'd teach me guy stuff, you know. He kinda made me into a tomboy, I guess you could say. He always said that he didn't have any boys of his own so he wanted me to be the boy. And I kinda really liked it." Kelly's stepfather did not "make" her into a "tomboy" but, rather, the gender relations and overall interaction at home led Kelly to reflexively embody such an accountably subordinate masculinity to her stepfather's dominating masculinity. For example, one aspect of "doing masculinity" in the family that Kelly relished was practicing certain gendered privileges. Kelly explains how the special bond with her stepfather empowered her to embody such privileges:

> I could be messy and my sisters couldn't. And they had to keep their room clean and I didn't. They had to do dishes and help my mom with stuff. I could just throw my clothes on the floor and they couldn't. Oh, and when we were eating dinner in front of the TV, it was only my stepfather and me. My sisters and Mom had to eat at the kitchen table. And I'd like just watch him, you know. When he'd be finished he'd just throw his plate to the side and he'd look at me and he'd go like, "You can, go ahead." And I'd throw my plate to the side like he did.

Kelly's stepfather ordered her older sister and mother to pick up after Kelly. The two never protested because "If they did, he'd come down on them. My sister hated me for that, and I think my mom did too."

Although Kelly had no desire to work in a factory like her stepfather, she nevertheless chose to do what he did at home because they seemed to be the "fun things." Kelly's stepfather taught her how to ride a dirt bike, a four-wheeler, and a snowmobile. The two watched sports together, such as the New England Patriots football games on TV, and "We tossed the football around a lot." Neither sister engaged in these types of bodily practices and interaction with their stepfather.

Confronting structured patriarchal gender relations at home, then, Kelly reflexively deliberated the advantages and benefits of being "Daddy's boy," as this allowed her, for example, to "be messy," to avoid domestic labor, and to escape the repercussions of her stepfather's physical violence and verbal abuse. Accordingly, Kelly became accountably masculine—"I just decided I didn't want to act like a girl, it was more fun to act boyish." Thus, a principal requirement of her at-home masculinity entailed reflexively distancing herself from all that is feminine. In fact, Kelly "hated" to dress and act like a girl. For example, she disliked dresses because they made it difficult to play sports and climb trees, and they would inevitably become "all torn up by the end of the day from playing outside with boys." Eventually her mother stopped pressuring her to "dress like a girl," and she has since worn baggy jeans, work boots, sweatshirts, and occasionally a duckbill hat. Kelly decided it made life easier to dress "like a boy" and it was "more fun to act like a boy because I could do anything I wanted. My stepfather even taught me that it was okay to burp out loud. He taught me how to make a mess and that it was okay to fart out loud whenever I wanted." Kelly thus embodied localized subordinate masculine display and practices—including certain bodily emissions—and reflexively distanced herself from the femininity of her mother and sisters because:

> They would always be wearing clean clothes and making sure they look okay. My mother and my sisters have to wear dresses, cook for people, clean up, and stuff like that. Who wants to do that shit? It was just stupid. Girls are wimps. They aren't very strong. They do boring stuff, and they're afraid of everything. They hear a noise and they are like—ah, you know. It's just stupid.

I asked Kelly if her mother was a role model for her in any way. She responded:

> Not at all. She would kiss my boo-boos but I didn't want to end up like her, you know. She just has like a real boring life, you know. She's a fucking drunk and she just let my stepfather like push her around. She'd always do what he told her or she'd get beat up and there wasn't nothin' she could do about it. What kinda life is that? I did what my stepfather did 'cause it was fun to do guy stuff, you know, and I looked up to him.

Reflexively rejecting femininity and embodying a localized and accountable subordinate masculinity in relation to her stepfather's dominating masculinity also provided Kelly power through violence. For example, when I asked Kelly whether it bothered her that her stepfather physically abused her mother, she responded that her mother "had it comin', 'cause she always hassled my stepfather, you know. She got what she deserved." Kelly defined her mother as a "hassle" to her stepfather because she "just got drunk all the time, give him shit, not do anything around the house, just lazy, you know." In contrast, Kelly looked up to her stepfather because "he taught me all kinds of things and he didn't take no shit from my mom. So that had a lot of influence on me, you know. My mom didn't really care about me, you know, but my stepfather did." Despite this endorsement of violence and her embodied subordinate masculinity, Kelly was never a victim of assaultive or sexual violence, nor did she ever engage in these crimes, at home.

School, Street, and Assaultive Violence

Through sixth grade, Kelly enjoyed school, had a few friends, got along well with teachers, and maintained a C average. Kelly considered that she and her friends (mostly boys) were the jocks at school, who never did anything wrong and had great fun together playing sports on the playground. Kelly described the structure of girls' groups at school as involving primarily the "preppies" and the "badass" as well as a variety of not-so-distinct girl groups. The preppies were the most dominant popular girl group. The jocks were not organized into a specific group; they "just played sports together." As Kelly notes, "Us jocks hung out with all kinds of people." The remaining "not-so-distinct" groups represented different versions of subordinate femininities of the in-school girl clique hierarchy.

Despite the above, in the seventh grade Kelly became a loner because her friends had suddenly rejected her. And often she was the victim of verbal bullying: "I would get bullied, mostly by the jocks, for the clothes I would wear and because I shaved the back of my head. My clothes weren't up to fashion and they started to call me names 'cause I looked like a boy, you know, and acted like a boy. So I'd get picked on about that. And my old friends would always be talking behind my back."

Kelly explained that she reflexively chose to wear "boys clothes" because it "was easier to do boy stuff and I didn't want to look like a girl, you know." Kelly also decided to shave the back of her head and wear a duck-bill sports hat to further enhance her effort to avoid "looking like a girl." Kelly's friends did not have a problem with her overall "boyish" embodiment, but when she shaved the back of her head they began to reject her, and the girls in particular talked behind her back: "They'd stare at me and then whisper stuff to each other. Then they'd walk by me and call me a 'dyke,' and then they'd all laugh. And once someone drew a picture of me looking like a guy with a big dick, and they put it on my gym locker." Kelly was also subjected to peer abuse by the dominant masculine boys who often called her a wimp, told her that she "was a fucking girl," and bellowed at her to "stop acting like a guy 'cause you can't do guy stuff." Thus, Kelly experienced peer interaction that accentuated the impropriety of her gender display and practices as a girl and as a boy—she embodied a subordinate masculinity and these bullying incidents momentarily established a hierarchical hegemonic relationship between the bullies and Kelly. In short, because Kelly was the sole female jock who dressed in such a manner, she reflexively attributed her peers' perception of her shaved head as "going too far for them." I asked Kelly how she decided to respond to this development:

> It really bothered me for awhile that my old girlfriends turned against me. I felt confused and didn't know what to do. So I stopped playing sports 'cause I didn't want to be around them, I didn't want to be called names, you know. But after a while I knew that they just wanted to be popular, you know. And I hated the popular preppy girls. All they care about is their faces, their ass, and boys. They're wimps and they just do all this boring stuff. My old girlfriends just wanted to be like them and I didn't.

What especially and continually concerned Kelly was verbal bullying by the dominant boys, particularly being told she was a "wimp," allegedly unfit to do "guy stuff." As Kelly stated: "That really bothered me the most, 'cause I didn't like being hassled, but I couldn't fight like guys do. I kinda felt like a wimp when guys would like hassle me, you know, about that." Because of her physical size—Kelly was shorter than most of the boys who verbally abused her—she lacked confidence in "fighting back," as the masculine culture of the school dictated. Consequently, Kelly decided to talk with her stepfather about the peer abuse at school, "And he said I needed to threaten the boys, you know. To go after the boys, not the girls, so everyone can see me, you know. To do it so kids could see. Like, 'You keep it up and I'll take you down.' And then when they [boys and girls] saw what I did to a couple of guys at school they just left me alone."

After reflexively deciding to approach her stepfather, he told her to threaten the boys because if they "backed down," the girls would likewise stop abusing her. Kelly explained to her stepfather that she felt ill-prepared physically to threaten the boys who verbally abused her. Thus, Kelly's stepfather taught her specifically how, as Kelly put it, to "fight like a guy": "He taught me that being short made me faster, you know. He said the lower you are to the ground the faster you are. He taught me how I had that advantage, you know." Kelly and her stepfather would "play fight," and he taught her to "scrooch down when he'd swing a punch at me. And then I'd just swipe his feet out from under him or tackle him. My stepfather taught me that. And then he told me to punch them in the face." Kelly used this method of fighting in response to verbal bullying by boys at school. The following is a representative example:

> One day a kid [a boy] walked by me in the hall at school and called me a wimp. He said I was just a "fucking girl," like that. Just a "girl," you know. He'd been hasslin' me like that, sayin' stuff like that, that I couldn't fight, you know. So I was tired of him, you know what I mean? So I decided to fight him right there in the hall. I wanted kids to see what I could do, you know. I ended up breaking his jaw. And I got excused for one day, and then I got to come back the next day.

I asked Kelly if this boy was physically bigger or smaller than her:

> He was a little bigger but I knew I could take him. I felt I could take care of myself—I was shorter but stronger than a lot of kids. I thought about what my stepfather told me and kids kept sayin', "You're not gonna take any shit, are ya?" And so I did it to him. There were lots a kids around, so I ran up to him and just liked tackled him, you know. I mean I real fast like got down on him and just grabbed his legs and pulled him down. He didn't even try to hit me. He just laid right there and let me pound on his face. He kinda seemed afraid to fight back, you know.

Kelly told her stepfather about the fight; he was "real proud" that she "didn't take any shit from this kid." I then asked Kelly if she was involved in other fights at school and she said: "Oh, yeah. After that anyone who called me names like 'wimp' or 'fucking girl.' They thought they were bigger and better than I was. So I proved them wrong. I'd take them down and pound on them with my fists and slam their head on the floor and tell them to shut the fuck up. And they would."

Kelly never fought girls at school, only boys. She participated in "about three dozen fights at school and I'd always win the fights with guys. Because of that I didn't need to fight girls. They saw what I could do and so they just left me alone. I was someone not to mess with, you know." Kelly's old jock girlfriends stopped verbally abusing her as well, and she carefully chose her battles with boys:

> There are a lot of guys that are bigger than me and I wouldn't fight them, you know. Just guys kinda my size. Lots a times I'd just beat the shit out of guys before they'd say anything. Just go up to them and smash them in the face and say, "You better keep your mouth shut," you know, like that. But the big jocks and stuff, and the preppies, the popular guys, I just left them alone 'cause they didn't want anything to do with me anyway. So it was just other guys my size that I took down. So they wouldn't try to give me shit.

Despite her assaultive violence, Kelly remained marginal-ized at school as subordinate "Other" by both dominant boys and girls. Although Kelly continued to be a loner, she did gain some masculine confidence and respect at school—she "han-dled" each conflictual situation in a personal and individual way; she specifically targeted boys her "size" prior to any verbal bullying; and she was accorded, to a certain extent, the deference she felt she deserved. That is, through her masculine (albeit sub-ordinate) presence at school, the boys who verbally bullied her (or may do so) eventually stopped because Kelly either "took them down" or threatened to do so.

Subsequently, in eighth grade Kelly reflexively decided to "hang out" on the street with some "badass guys." The badass boys, according to Kelly, frequently challenged the authority of the school (some even physically fought teachers); they regularly "skipped class" and "beat up people" at school, and on the street they engaged in robberies, burglaries, and group violence. Kelly chose to join this group because "I didn't have any friends. And they liked to do what I liked to do. And they accepted me 'cause I'm a good fighter. They were doing things like I'd seen all my life. They liked to party and get drunk, and didn't take any shit from anyone. And that was normal to me." The "badass guys" Kelly decided to join formed a group in which she was "the only girl who 'hung' with the guys. I was the only one that didn't dress like a girl and didn't act like a girl. All the other girls who would hang with us wore really tight jeans and sexy tops." Kelly referred to these girls as "slutty badass girls" because "they had slept with like over a hundred guys." Kelly "hung out" with the guys (not the girls) but never engaged in sexuality with these guys because, as she put it:

> I would have sex with them if they wanted. But they don't treat me that way, you know. I'm one of them, you could say. I'd get called "ladybug" because female and male ladybugs look the same and act the same. I just got the nickname "la-dybug" because I was a girl that acted like a boy. So we never talk about sex and they never come on to me and I don't come on to them.

Kelly went on to say that she was not a virgin but only had sex a few times because "sex is not that important to me." Kelly considered herself heterosexual—"I ain't no dyke"—and earlier had become sexually active around age twelve with several jock boyfriends who introduced her to heterosexuality—this is when she began to take up a heterosexual project. Kelly also had several "lovers" who were not in school and were considerably older than her. However, since breaking away from the "jock crowd," Kelly was now celibate and seemed comfortable with this since she otherwise was accepted by the "badass boys."

I then asked Kelly if the "slutty badass girls" fought boys like she did, and she responded: "No way, they only fight girls. And so that kinda raised my status 'cause I would fight boys, just go after boys for no reason, you know." The slutty badass girls fought girls "mostly over shit I couldn't care about, you know. They'd give each other shit about the way they looked and then fight about it." These girls never "hassled" Kelly because "They're afraid of me, you know. They know what would happen if they did. So they didn't mess with me." Moreover, these girls rarely "hung out" with Kelly and the guys but, rather, "They'd go walking around stores and the mall. Or they'd sit down, listen to music, get high. And that was about it. They never really did anything with the guys except fuck them, you know."

Instead of going to the mall and engaging in sexuality, Kelly chose to play video games with the guys, wrestle with them, throw a football around with them, and occasionally she would "go out driving" and "stompin'" with them. Eventually Kelly decided to "strut" like the boys. As she pointed out: "I'd walk like them, you know. Kinda big steps with my arms hangin' down and my shoulders swaying back and forth. They liked that and I got called 'ladybug' for it." Kelly noted that her gait was quite different from the slutty badass girls because "They walked like girls, you know, with their butts tight, and short steps, standin' straight up, like that." Another embodied masculine practice Kelly reflexively chose to participate in on the street—but the "slutty badass girls" did not—was "power barfs," which she described as follows: "Let's see. You drink beer and salt, and you'd gargle it in your mouth until it gets all foamy and then you swallow it. And then someone would hit you in the stomach and you just puke it all up. And the biggest splash and mess is the winner."

Because Kelly reflexively decided to join in many of the same activities practiced by the boys in the group, she "was seen as a girl, but cool like a guy": "I wasn't a guy, but I was in the guy group. Most of the time whenever the guys did something, I was there and they didn't mind it, 'cause I wasn't a bitchy type of person, you know, like every single girl is. Plus I could do what they do, you know."

Although Kelly embodied a subordinate masculinity at school and on the street in the badass group, she did not "pass" as a "male." Kelly had more status in the badass group than the "slutty badass girls," yet she nevertheless was subordinate to both the preppy boys at school and the badass boys at school and on the street. As Kelly expressed her relationship with the latter boys: "The guys would always tell me what to do 'cause I'm a girl, you know. They'd say I don't know shit, and stuff like that, you know. A lot of guys are sexist and didn't want me around a lot." Kelly further reflects on these boys' situationally constructed form of hegemonic masculinity:

Q. How were they sexist?

A. You know. They'd think that 'cause they're guys they are tougher and better. But I can beat the shit out of a lot of the guys. But they got to do things I didn't.

Q. Can you give me an example?

A. Ah, you know. Like they always got to go on robberies and burglaries, you know, and stompin', just 'cause they're guys.

Q. You didn't always participate when the boys were involved in those crimes?

A. No, 'cause sometimes they thought I'd get hurt, and then they'd have to deal with me. I'd get in the way and stuff like that, you know, when they gonna use knives, guns, and base-ball bats.

Gender Conformity and Nonviolence at Home

What do these two life stories teach us about the relationship among sex, gender, sexuality, and nonviolence in the home setting? Beginning with Lenny, we "see" him confronting the constraints and possibilities established through patriarchal gender relations at home, and his active adoption of certain forms of social action. Lenny's embodied practices at home articulated primarily with those of his father—his favorite things to do were activities he and "Dad" did together, such as hunting, fishing, playing catch, and playing darts. These represent the salient available practices in the home milieu that Lenny engaged in. Accordingly, Lenny embodied a subordinate masculinity as he benefited from gender privilege, yet was simultaneously subordinated to his dominating masculine father in this setting. He primarily oriented his actions for his father's approval, and given that Lenny successfully engaged in such practices— Lenny's father was "real proud" of him when he shot his first deer—his masculinity never was challenged in this milieu by his father or by others. Lenny was accountably masculine at home as he engaged in situationally normative masculine conduct that aligned with his male appearance, and such embodied masculinity helped reproduce in-home gender relations; Lenny was an accountable gender conformist in this setting, and sexuality was in essence a nonissue and thus was not salient in the home setting. Distancing himself from the feminine practices of his mother and sister (who performed the vast majority of domestic labor), Lenny confidently and for the most part unreflexively embodied a masculine presence and *place* at home and developed a close relationship with his father through kindred embodied interaction that seemed smooth, uneventful, socially coordinated, and nonviolent.

Kelly was similar to Lenny in that she actively rejected femininity; she did so, however, for a different reason—practicing femininity was painfully confining and required unexciting domestic labor. Accordingly, in her negotiation of patriarchal gender relations at home, Kelly reflexively distanced herself from in-home emphasized feminine practices (as represented by her sisters and mother), even to the extent of discounting her mother as a mentor: for Kelly, her mother was an intoxicated and weak person living a lackluster life. There was, however, an additional advantage from Kelly's point of view: eschewing femininity and practicing masculinity permitted Kelly to enjoy tranquil (rather than tumultuous) interaction with her stepfather. For Kelly, then, practicing femininity restricted bodily mobility and freedom; practicing masculinity offered a semblance of autonomous self-rule in the home when compared to the status of her sisters and mother. Although Kelly's interaction at home and alliance with her stepfather clearly included tension and fear, she reflexively allied with her stepfather in part to avoid succumbing to his violence and to avoid being rendered "weak" like her mother. While enjoying greater privileges than her mother and sisters, Kelly remained subordinate to, and under the power of, her dominating masculine stepfather. Kelly's reflexive negotiation in this setting was different from Lenny's in part because of the presence of patriarchal violence.

Through intimate attachment to her stepfather, then, Kelly actually became accountably "Daddy's boy" and reaped the gendered benefits such embodied social action promised. Arguably, Kelly reflexively drew on the practices at home and, like Lenny, constructed a subordinate masculinity in this setting that simultaneously benefitted from the oppression of her sisters and her mother. Kelly was accountable to—and wholly endorsed—her stepfather's in-home hegemonic masculine project. Yet Kelly's path to masculinity was not the smooth social process that Lenny experienced, primarily because of the imbalance between her female appearance and masculine behavior. Given her explicit renunciation of femininity, Kelly's mother, for example, consistently pressured her to "act" and "dress like a girl"—Kelly's "sex" is focused on by her mother to disparage her gender behavior. Nevertheless, Kelly uniformly struggled against her mother's efforts and seamlessly subverted femininity. Additionally, because of the stable and substantial support of the person in power—the stepfather (who exercised his ability to overrule her mother)—Kelly's sex and gender imbalance was situationally erased: The stepfather *honored* Kelly above all other family members as "Daddy's boy," and thus his power situationally rendered invisible any sex-gender asymmetry. Kelly's stepfather held her account-able to masculine embodiment and she did not resist. In fact, Kelly literally *became* "Daddy's boy," and this gender embodi-ment eventually was normalized in this setting. Although Kelly's stepfather practiced hegemonic masculinity in relation to her mother and sisters, in relation to Kelly her stepfather constructed a dominating masculinity. Kelly also practiced nonviolent masculinity at home: She had no need to engage in violence because her stepfather recognized and respected her masculinity. Moreover, like Lenny, sexuality was fundamen-tally a nonissue for Kelly in the home setting and therefore was not salient to her interactions and practices. Consequently, Kelly occupied a specific subordinate masculine presence and *place* in in-home gender relations as an accountably gender conformist.

Repression, Reflexivity, and Recognition

Both Lenny and Kelly grew up in homes whereby they were considered "gender conformists" and neither personally expe-rienced assaultive or sexual violence victimization nor did they engage in any form of violence in this setting. In contrast, within the setting of the school, a social process developed involving repression, reflexivity, and recognition and that resulted in both being labeled "gender deviants" and subsequently both engaged in assaultive violence. Let me briefly outline this social process and thus pathway to assaultive violence.

Repression

Both Lenny and Kelly experienced peer interaction in the social setting of the school that oppressively accentuated a very specific type of verbal and social bullying that centered on the body and featured a perceived imbalance between sex category and gender behavior. What these interview data show is that the meaning assigned by the in-school bullies to Lenny's and Kelly's *gender behavior* is influenced through their *perceived sex category*. In other words, for both Lenny and Kelly, because their sex category was judged to be incongruent with their gender behavior, they subsequently became victims of gender repression through consistent bullying.

For Lenny, there was an imbalance between his perceived male category and his alleged unmanly behavior and body (e.g., he did not "fight back"; he did not play sports; and he had a pudgy, soft, and smooth "feminine" body). In other words, Lenny's alleged feminine body size and shape and bodily behavior were viewed by the in-school bullies as controverting his perceived (male) sex category. According to the bullies, Lenny was a "wimp" and thereby he "failed" to accomplish hegemonic masculinity in terms of appropriate bodily display and practice. Yet, because he was identified as a "male," he was consistently repressed through bullying victimization.

For Kelly, both the girls and the boys attempted through their bullying to invalidate her masculine display and practice because of her female sex category. Kelly's sex category was viewed by the bullies to disparage her gender display (e.g., calling her a "dyke") and her gender behavior (e.g., she allegedly was a "wimp" who could not do "guy stuff" because she is "a girl"). According to the bullies, then, because Kelly "failed" in terms of sex category rather than in bodily practice (she actually "beat up" numerous boys), she was the victim of gender repression through consistent bullying. And with Kelly we clearly discern the intersection of gender and sexuality: the contextually subordinate sexual term "dyke" is ascribed to her (by girls) for not practicing "proper" heterofemininity.

For both Lenny and Kelly, then, their *body* and their *bodily behavior* conveyed a sex/gender combined image at school that the bullies viewed as an imbalance between sex category and gender behavior; at home both were considered "gender conformists," yet at school they were now labeled "gender deviants." And it was this situationally recognized bodily imbalance by the bullies at school—as conveyed through their verbal and social bullying—that *motivated* Lenny and Kelly to engage in reflexivity, to which we now turn.

Reflexivity

Through reflexivity, both Lenny and Kelly realized initially that their bodies *restrained* their agency: they could not live up to the in-school masculine expectations of physically fighting back when verbally bullied. This was extremely distressing to both of them, as they felt small and subordinated in front of peers; accordingly, they both reflexively concluded they must be "wimps." In other words, Lenny's and Kelly's bodies were actually participating in their reflexive agency by suggesting possible courses of social action. Although Lenny and Kelly internally decided they wanted to respond "appropriately" to the verbal bullying, they realized through reflexivity the limits of their embodied action. So Lenny, initially, decided to run home immediately after school; Kelly, simply chose to "put up" with the bullying. Frustrated, and given the continual distressing situation, they both entered into an intensified reflexivity and decided to turn to their father/stepfather for help. And both learned when and how to use their bodies in an accountably masculine fashion. For both Lenny and Kelly, then, their bodies became objects of their reflexive social action. Lenny, given specific directions when to use his body, was advised, in particular, to "pick the battles you can win." And Kelly's body became the object of her social action as she attempted to transform it into a masculine force "appropriate" to her specific school setting.

During this intensified reflexivity, then, both Lenny and Kelly came to internally conceptualize themselves in the way that others perceived them—they reified the images communicated by others. Much of this internal conceptualization was arrived at by way of interaction and communication with others. Through such interaction and communication, both Lenny and Kelly took an "external" view of themselves, thus becoming the objects of their own reflexivity. Because of the shame and mortification they suffered from bullying victimization, an assault upon their self-definition and social identification emerged. This assault drove them to move from a tacit relationship with their bodies to a more conscious and enhanced reflexive one. In other words, they internalized the "external" by engaging in reflexivity; in the process, they both, through internal conversations, determined their courses of action in relation to their bodies and to their social circumstances.

In short, Lenny and Kelly reflexively deliberated about their individual social circumstances at school—which were significantly different from their interactions at home—and, in particular, they reflected on their bodies to determine what they could and could not "do" in the school setting to overcome their subordinating social situations. Accordingly, their bodies became reflexive participants in the generating and shaping of their social practices.

Recognition

Extending his reflexivity into social action, Lenny responded to "being bullied" by internally deciding to create an opportunity in which he could be a "bully"—he attempted to use what little physical power he possessed to harm someone less powerful and weaker. Shame and inadequacy threatened Lenny's masculine self as revealed in his reflexivity. Electing to verbally bully and physically assault the "high water" was an attempt to validate some type of masculine self for his audience and for himself—compensatory in the sense of attempting to reduce/offset the subordinating interactions and feelings produced at school. Lenny sought compensation—rather than social power—by going after the "high water" rather than the bullies, seeking to define himself as normally masculine in the eyes of others. He reflexively hoped his body would facilitate masculine agency and eradicate the "wimp" label. But his audience failed him. Predictably, he remained subordinated at school because of a socially identified imbalance between sex category and gender behavior. He was subjected continually to derogatory verbal bullying, all of which reinforced his feelings of masculine inadequacy. Indeed, his body continued to *restrain* his masculine agency in the in-school social setting—thus Lenny remained a "gender deviant" at school.

Realizing he was unable to embody masculinity at school—because the "high water" was the only boy he could "beat up"—Lenny reflexively decided to restrict his effort at masculine recognition to his neighborhood. Because the behavioral expressions activated by the contextual bullying at school could now be directed only outside the school situation, he had to move to another "site" to become accountably masculine. In other words, Lenny's embodied interaction at school directed him toward courses of masculine social action that were realizable physically and that could be accomplished outside the boundaries of school. Lenny had a desperate need to abandon his "feminized" position and to fit into the dominant masculine model offered by the "cool tough guys" at school. For Lenny, then, the dominant masculine practices and thus in-school discursive criteria were not rejected. Rather, physical subordination directed him toward reflexively fixating on a specific site, his neighborhood, and on a particular form of body deployment, assaultive violence, where such practices—and thus a balance between sex appearance and gender behavior—could be realized. Moreover, Lenny had access to less-powerful people in his neighborhood and therefore to the means by which his body could attain dominating physical expression. Given that Lenny was removed from any type of recognized and embodied masculine status in school—he was even criticized verbally for assaulting the "high water"—interaction (sometimes violent) with the available younger and smaller boys in his neighborhood was especially attractive, and became a powerful means of embodying dominating masculinity in the street setting.

In attempting to masculinize his body within the captivating criteria of "cool tough guy" dominant masculinity, Lenny engendered a powerful sense of self by "taking charge" on his neighborhood street and by conquering younger and smaller boys' bodies through assaultive violence. It was in the setting of the neighborhood street that Lenny's body took on a relatively new size and shape (he is physically larger and stronger than the younger boys), where it moved in a different way than at school (he was physically competent and dominant in this setting), and where it established inevitably a novel image for

Lenny through the way he presented himself to the neighbor-hood boys and how he was "read" eventually by these boys. By concentrating his interactional efforts within the context of the neighborhood, Lenny was able to transform how he interacted with and through his body: he now constructed a dominating masculinity *in this setting* because his male appearance and masculine behavior were aligned; he validated his "sex" through his "gender" behavior. Lenny was living his body in a new way, as force and power were now embodied in him—whereas at school neither existed—and he took on a new *place* in the power hierarchy among boys and, therefore, a new embodied self in the setting of the street. His reflexive choice to be violent in his neighborhood was a situational resource in which Lenny could be powerful through bodily practice—he embodied a dominating masculine presence in the street setting. Lenny reflexively created a situation entailing new gender relations among boys, in which he was in masculine control and in which he could not be criticized and rejected by a subordinating audience. In short, Lenny constructed a nonthreatening gendered context in which masculinity could be performed according to the in-school dominant criteria. In the brief, illusory moment of each assaultive violent incident against smaller and younger neighborhood boys who challenged his heteromasculinity (e.g., calling him a fag), Lenny felt morally justified in reacting through assaultive violence. And in the process, the subordinated became the dominating because his male appearance and gender behavior now complemented each other. In short, Lenny's behavior on the street constructed a new meaning assigned to his sex and it influenced the nature of his overall interaction with the neighborhood boys—he now gained *recognition* as a gender conformist.

Turning to Kelly, her newly developed bodily skills allowed her to respond to oppressive verbal bullying by attempting to make use of opportunities where physical domination of boys would be viewed by others—she reflexively resolved to target boys she knew she could "take down." Kelly used physically violent power to intimidate others, likewise seeking compensation rather than social power. She, too, reflexively sought to eradicate any "wimp" label so as to avoid being bullied. And Kelly succeeded—to a point.

Kelly's body now *facilitated* masculine agency, an agency that constructed a more confident sense of self, a new way of interacting with and through her body in the school setting. Kelly reflexively opted to attempt to construct a new gendered self through her embodied practices at school, and she was successful, as force and power were to a certain extent now embodied in her practices. Kelly literally possessed a different body and a new gendered self (e.g., a don't-t-mess-with-me demeanor). Kelly not only practiced a new and specific kind of bodily skill, she also embodied a new moral and emotional universe—exhibiting particular bodily talent as well as appropriating proper emotional attitudes to accompany and foster embodied masculine success; body and mind—skill and attitude—were indivisible here (see Wacquant 2004). Kelly literally created a particular way of incarnating masculinity in and through her body.

Despite her actual and successful accomplishment of masculine practices, however, and because of the continued imbalance between her sex appearance and gender behavior, Kelly (as Lenny) remained considerably subordinated and marginalized at school. And because Kelly's perceived sex category continued to influence the meaning assigned to her bodily display and behavior, she was conceptualized at school (as was Lenny) as a "gender deviant." Because she had no friends, Kelly became a loner in the in-school social setting.

Turning to the badass street group for social acceptance and recognition, Kelly did not position herself as a "slutty badass girl" but, rather, attempted to become "one of the guys" (Miller 2001). Kelly's embodied practices—such as engaging in assaultive violence against boys, participating in "power barfs," and performing the appropriate "strut"—minimized gender difference, all the while maintaining a female appearance. Moreover, Kelly occasionally would be included—alongside the boys—in "stompin'," or group assaultive violence against other groups of boys. Nevertheless, and in a similar manner at school, perception of her female sex ensured that Kelly's experience as a masculine badass-group member could never be the same as the boys'. Given that dominant masculinity in the badass group was based in part on being physically tough, using the body as a weapon, and constructing a don't-mess-with-me demeanor, Kelly successfully used her body in these ways yet she had no intention to "pass" completely as male. Indeed, as at school, the badass boys perceived a female body under all the masculine display and practice. Thus, Kelly was deemed inadequate by the boys for specific activities, such as robberies, burglaries, and certain forms of stompin'. Kelly's sex appearance influenced the ultimate meaning assigned to her behavior by the badass boys and the nature of the overall social interaction between Kelly and these boys. Kelly's interaction on the street once again illustrates the reliance on both sex appearance and gender practices in validating sex or gender. In other words, since Kelly's sex appearance did not align with her gender behavior—and such nonalignment was accentuated by those in power—her masculine practices were not simply questioned but also were subordinated, and she never did gain full *recognition* as a gender conformist.

I will have more to say about Lenny and Kelly in chapter 6. For now, let us turn to chapter 4 where I present two sex-offender life histories.

4

Sexual Violence

Sam and Kristen

Chapter 4 focuses on a white working-class boy and girl involved in sexual violence: Sam and Kristen (both pseudonyms). Sam and Kristen were chosen specifically from the larger pool of interviewees for four explicit reasons. First, both Sam and Kristen grew up in homes where neither personally experienced assaultive or sexual violence. Thus, these two case studies facilitate comparison as to why a boy and a girl eventually engaged in sexual violence despite growing up in a home in which they were not physically or sexually victimized. Second, Sam (male sex category) and Kristen (female sex category) represent different embodied sexes and genders—masculinity (Sam) and femininity (Kristen)—and therefore typify two significantly different sexed and gendered pathways into sexual violence. Third, Kristen engaged in sexual violence outside the home; Sam engaged in sexual violence exclusively at home. I discuss why Sam and Kristen engaged in sexual violence in different settings and how the particular embodied action is related to heteromasculinity and heterofemininity. Finally, the two case studies are nicely juxtaposed because both Sam and Kristen grew up in the same neighborhood and attended the same school at the same time. Accordingly, this chapter reports data as to why a boy and a girl from the *same* social milieu engaged in sexual violence for both similar and different reasons and in different settings. We begin this chapter with Sam.

Sam

Sam was a short, overweight, boyish-looking eighteen-year-old with short blond hair who was markedly animated while articulating his life story. He wore a bright-blue youth-prison "jump suit" with "slippers" on his feet to both interviews, and he was so excited about telling me his story that he came to the interviews with detailed lists of important episodes and circumstances in his life. He also pointed out at several stages in our conversations that the interviews helped him understand the past and that he hoped his story would help others. Sam was incarcerated for sexual violence against two young girls. In what follows, I describe through Sam's words his family relations, and eventually sexual violence, at home.

Family Relations

Sam was from a working-class suburb where he lived with his two adoptive parents and younger biological sister. Like other members of the "respectable" working class, the family owned its own home when Sam was growing up. Sam became a member of this family when he and his sister were abandoned by their biological mother.

Sam and his sister were assigned to a variety of foster homes, eventually being adopted by his current foster parents when Sam was five. When Sam was younger, his "mom" and "dad" (what he calls them) worked at a service-industry job and a skilled manual job, respectively, generating a modest working-class income. Sam's mother did all the cooking at home, as well as the shopping for food and other necessities. The kids helped their mother with daily household cleaning. Their father, according to Sam, "mowed the lawn, loafed around, and worked with his tools."

Sam thus grew up among explicit practices defining "men's work" and "women's work" at home and in the workplace. Further, these practices nourished Sam's idea of future labor force participation: Sam reflexively decided that he wanted to "work with tools" after finishing high school. Indeed, by the time he was in high school Sam had his own automobile that was just as "decked out as Dad's."

Sam reported substantial family cohesiveness and stability, describing very close contact with both parents: "We went on many vacations together as a family—going camping, fishing, and hunting. We had a great time together." Sam indicated that he experienced an especially warm and affectionate family relationship (discipline was verbal, not physical) and remembered specifically bonding with his father: "He taught me all about tools and everything else, and I used to be able to hand him the tools when he was working on trailer trucks." Moreover, Sam's father had the power in the home: "Dad was the one who kept in control over everything." Sam's mother and the kids always yielded to his dad's decisions: "We always looked to Dad; he was the one who took control." Thus, Sam's father embodied a localized hegemonic masculinity and Sam's mother emphasized femininity.

Sam obviously identified with his father, who was his initial model for developing a specific type of maleness. Indeed, when I asked Sam if he was concerned about having approval from his father, he stated, "Yeah, that meant a lot to me, Dad telling me I did a good job helping him." Although Sam's father constructed a hegemonic masculinity in relation to his mother's emphasized femininity, in relation to Sam he practiced a dominating masculinity. Sam's interviews clearly show that within the family a substantial commitment toward, and a smooth reproduction of, a subordinate masculinity was constructed by Sam in relation to his father's dominating masculinity, and Sam's accountable subordinate masculinity included numerous practices such as working with tools, fishing and hunting, and manual labor. And Sam expanded his conception of masculinity at the time: "Success at work, power, money, strong, being like Dad." Sam never was the victim of violence at home nor did he ever engage in assaultive or sexual violence *against family members.* Thus, it was in this setting where Sam initially took up a project of masculinity as his own—he embodied localized (subordinate) masculine appearance and practices in this setting.

School Relations

At school Sam collided with an unsettling social situation. In elementary school, after breaking away from a group of "troublemakers," Sam was subjected to consistent verbal bullying because of his physical size and shape (he was shorter and heavier than the other boys), eventually to the extent of "living in fear of going to school." Sam did not do well in school because, according to him, he reflexively worried more about being verbally bullied than doing schoolwork and was placed in special-education courses. During his eighth-grade year, he recalled, "Everybody looked at me like 'Oh, there is something wrong with him.'"

Being verbally bullied about shortness and obesity and feeling rejection for being "slow" intellectually extended through eighth grade and into high school. Although Sam observed numerous instances of boys fighting at school because of bullying, he reflexively decided not to respond directly to the bullies because of his physical size—he did not want to be "beat up." As a result, Sam constantly watched his back, watched where he was stepping, "always really nervous at school, because people picked on me." When asked if he discussed the bullying with his parents, Sam replied:

> Yeah, I talked to my dad about it. My dad kept telling me to fight back, let them know I was a tough guy. He would tell me: "Hit them right back. Don't let them get to you, don't let them bug you." And I wanted to fight back but I didn't feel like I was strong, like I could fight back like Dad said.

Thus Sam reflexively mulled over ongoing embarrassment in school for poor grades and for being a "special-ed kid." He had internal conversations about bodily inadequacy because of his physical size and shape, as well as a sense of powerlessness for his inability to fight back as his father recommended and as his peers expected. Consequently, Sam decided to become a loner at school and he chose to stop discussing the bullying with his father because he did not want to disappoint him. As he states:

> They would call me "porky," a "wimp," that I couldn't stick up for myself, that I was a "mama's boy." I wasn't worth anything according to them. I felt like I was a girl, someone they [the popular boys] shouldn't hang around or talk to. So, of course I didn't tell Dad, and my loner lifestyle . . .

The boys who bullied Sam were "the popular ones," dominant boys who played sports, attended parties, and had lots of friends. When I asked Sam how they identified him as a "wimp," he replied that they would "try to get me to fight with them. They would say, 'Come on fat boy, fight.' But they were all tall and strong so I'd run away. I wouldn't stay around them. And they'd call me names." Thus, like Lenny and Kelly, a fleeting hegemonic masculinity was established through the bullies-Sam relationship. And during his internal conversations, Sam decided he wanted to fight back like other kids, and as his father had taught him, but eventually he concluded that he was not strong enough. Consequently, Sam did not have any friends at school: "I wasn't like one of them; I wasn't one that had friends to hang out with."

Sam clearly was reflexively questioning his ability to protect himself from the ongoing "degradation ceremonies" at school, unable to control such a threatening environment. In fact, he internally viewed himself as incapable of making the appropriate masculine response—fighting back physically—which he had learned through interaction at school and from his special mentor (father). And significantly, he decided he could not discuss this situation with his parents because he determined that he would "let them down" for not being able to handle the situation as his father instructed. Thus by the time he was fifteen years old, Sam lacked masculine resources and therefore reflexively he felt extremely powerless, distressed, and subordinate at school—he was unable to accountably construct dominant masculinity and thus he was seriously subordinated and feminized in this setting.

During his freshman year in high school Sam began to develop internal conversations consisting of sexually objectifying and desiring girls. He learned to objectify and desire girls from interaction at school and not from his parents. As Sam states: "Kids were talking at school about blow jobs, getting laid, telling dirty jokes, and about having sex and stuff like that." Sam constantly heard the dominant popular boys' "sex talk" about sexual objectification of girls as well as heterosexual exploits and experiences. He reflexively desired to participate in heterosexuality but, because he was a "virgin" and a loner, he concluded he could not share the "sex-talk" camaraderie. It was schoolboy chat, then, that was Sam's initial source of information about sexuality and thus his sexual awakening—in this setting Sam began to affix a heterosexual project to his ongoing attempt at a masculine project. So it was during his freshman year that Sam became very interested in heterosexuality: reflexively he decided that he also wanted to experience heterosexual relations to "learn what it was like." Clearly, this development had its gender component. When asked why he eventually decided that he wanted to experience sexuality, Sam added,

> I thought, well, I'm a guy, so this is something that every guy does, that I want to be part of this. I want to be like the other guys. I want to know what it feels like, I want to know what goes on.

Sam knew several girls at school with whom he wished to have a sexual relationship, but because of the constant bullying, "I didn't think I was good enough. I didn't have the trust enough to gain access to a girl. I didn't think any girl would be interested in me." Thus Sam reflexively objectified girls and wanted to develop sexual contact with girls in order to be "like the other guys," but through his internal conversations he determined that he was unable to fulfill this situationally defined dominant masculine criterion.

By age fifteen, then, Sam was experiencing degradation ceremonies at school about his physical size and shape, as well as earning poor grades. His inability to "fight back" internally haunted him and significantly added to his lack of masculine resources and accompanying negative masculine self-esteem.

This masculine insecurity was further enhanced by his inability to be a "real man" through developing the intensely sought-after sexual relationships with girls his age.

Sexual Violence at Home

Accordingly, Sam reflexively decided to attempt to overcome his lack of masculine resources and thereby diminish the negative masculine feelings and situations through controlling and manipulating behaviors involving the use of sexual power. Reflexively deciding that he was unable to be masculine by responding in a physically aggressive way to the people threatening him (i.e., the dominant "popular guys") and that he was incapable of developing sexual relationships with girls his age, Sam chose to turn to the masculine behaviors that were available to him—expressing control and power over younger girls through sexuality.

During his freshman year Sam began babysitting a few neighborhood girls (six to eight years old) in his house after school and then all day during the summer. It was Sam's idea to babysit and his parents instantly accepted, believing it was a splendid decision on Sam's part. During this year in high school—a time when he experienced most of the distressing events discussed earlier and when he "discovered" heterosexuality—Sam decided to begin sexually assaulting some of the girls he babysat:

> I wanted to have some kind of sexual experience. And that didn't happen at school. I mean, I wasn't around other people, I didn't experience relationships with people my own age. And I started seeing the girls I babysat as being innocent and being able to take advantage of easily. I looked at how my life was, how I feared the people at school, so I figured I could get a girl I was babysitting easier. That's why I wanted to babysit.

The adults trusted Sam with the girls because in front of them he had, through his internal conversations, decided to be gentle and caring toward them. The girls liked Sam, and thus he reflexively determined ways to gain their trust. Indeed, becoming a babysitter was a major turning point in Sam's life. As he interprets it: "Babysitting gave me a place where I was in control because I was taking care of kids and I had control over them." When asked how he chose specific girls to abuse, Sam explained that he noticed some of the girls were "more quiet" and more vulnerable, and therefore more easily exploitable.

Sam manipulated two of the girls into fondling him and performing oral sex on him for two years, reflexively deliberating about and deciding how to use specific strategies to gain access to them: "I kept gaining ways to manipulate, ways to like bribe, like act like I was helping them, act like I was doing good things for them, like playing games with them. For example, 'I'll play [video games] with you if you do this for me.'" Sam stated that he chose not to blatantly physically threaten the girls he sexually assaulted. Instead, he reflexively decided to "wrestle with them and throw them around, and pretend that I know all this self-defense stuff, making it look like I was invincible, like I was strong, tough, and couldn't be hurt. That they couldn't fight back. Through that, that's what I used to scare them."

The following extended dialogue reveals what the sexual violence accomplished for Sam:

> Q. How did it make you feel when you were able to manipulate the girls you were babysitting?
>
> A. I was getting away with something that nobody else that I saw was getting away with. I felt that I was number one. I felt like I was better, like I was a better person, because I could play this little game with them and they didn't see what was going on. Like, I could trap 'em. It was like then they really didn't have much of a choice but to go along with what I wanted them to do.
>
> Q. You felt special?
>
> A. Yeah, because it was like I could manipulate anybody, because it was like I could put on a facade like as if I was a good person all the time. I would be such a nice person. I went to church, I did things for people, I acted nice. I would paint the image like I was a good boy. And all the while I was having sex with these girls.

Q. How did it make you feel when you sexually assaulted these two girls?

A. I didn't feel like I was small anymore, because in my own grade, my own school, with people my own age, I felt like I was a wimp, the person that wasn't worth anything. But when I did this to the girls, I felt like I was big, I was in control of everything.

Q. And you continued to sexually assault these girls?

A. Yes, that's why I kept doing it, 'cause I felt that control and I wanted that control more and more and more. And that's why it was hard for me to stop, because I'd have to return to that old me of being small and not being anything. I wasn't good at sports, and tough and strong and stuff, so I wasn't fitting in with anybody that was really popular. I was like a small person, someone that nobody really paid attention to. I was the doormat at school. People walked all over me and I couldn't fight back.

Q. Did you feel you were entitled to these girls?

A. I felt like I should be able to have sexual contact with anybody that I wanted to. And I couldn't do that with girls my own age. So I felt like, okay, I'll get it from the girls I was babysitting.

Q. Why did you feel entitled to sex?

A. Like, well, I'm a guy. I'm supposed to have sex. I'm supposed to be like every other guy. And so I'm like them, but I'm even better than them [popular boys], because I can manipulate. They don't get the power and the excitement. They have a sexual relationship with a girl. She can say what she wants and she has the choice. But the girls I babysat didn't have the choice. It was like I made it look like they had a choice, but when they stated their choice, if they said no, I like bugged them and bugged them until they didn't say no.

Q. How did that make you feel in relation to the other males at school?

A. I was like better than every other guy, because there was no way I could get rejected. It was like, okay, they can have their relationships, I'm gonna do whatever I want. I'm better than they are.

Through this sexual violence, then, Sam actually constructed a hegemonic masculinity in relation to the girls he sexually violated—the violent interaction legitimated an unequal masculine/feminine relationship—while simultaneously convincing himself that he now represented *the* dominant masculinity among boys because through the commission of sexual violence his masculinity is now superior to the masculinity practiced by the "popular" boys at school.

Kristen

Kristen is a short, obese, and extremely talkative teenager with long dirty-blonde hair. To each interview she wore tight jeans, a tight T-shirt, high-heels, a stylish hairdo, and considerable makeup. Kristen spoke in a very straightforward and direct manner; at the time of the interviews she was incarcerated for serial sexual offending against a younger neighborhood boy. In what follows, I describe, through Kristen's own words, her family relations at home and eventually sexual violence outside both home and school.

Family Relations

Kristen was from a working-class community where she lived with her biological mother, her stepfather, and her younger twin sisters. The family rented a large apartment in the center of the city and Kristen met her biological father only once: "When I was twelve he came over and sat on the kitchen counter. That was scary 'cause he's a big man and I thought, wow, I never met him in my life and I thought, 'Wow, it's my dad.'" Unfortunately, this was the last time Kristen saw her father.

Kristen's stepfather was a factory worker and her mother was a homemaker. Kristen's mother did all the cooking at home, as well as the shopping for food and other necessities. Kristen helped her mother with daily household cleaning and "I did the dishes, took the trash out, and kept my room clean. Mom did everything else." When I asked Kristen what her stepfather did around the house she replied, "He sat on his butt, ate food, watched TV, and slept, 'cause he always said he was tired from working all day at the factory." Thus, Kristen grew up among explicit practices defining "men's work" and "women's work" at home and in the workplace, and Kristen's stepfather embodied a localized hegemonic masculinity and Kristen's mother, emphasized femininity.

For the most part, Kristen reported having a "good" family life as she indicates there was never any physical violence in the family and much cheerfulness and contentment overall. She was very close to her mother, especially prior to her twin sisters being born: "It was totally awesome. We did like absolutely everything together. I'd cry when Mom dropped me off at school because I didn't have my mommy. I had a great time with my mom." Kristen's relationship with her stepfather was "okay, but not like with Mom, we just didn't do much together."

Once the twins were born (when Kristen was eight years old) interaction at home began to change. On the weekends her mother often would leave the home and go grocery shopping or go to the mall, and according to Kristen, "It seemed like she was gone forever." Kristen would then be forced to stay home with the stepfather and the twins, and her stepfather increasingly demanded that Kristen babysit her sisters. "It was like he expected me to take care of them while he just laid on the couch and watched TV. And if I ever did anything wrong, he'd always call me 'stupid.' He kept saying that when Mom was gone." In fact, Kristen stated that her stepfather would only hug her twice a year: "On my birthday and at Christmas." Kristen provided me with another example of her father's occasional verbal abuse:

> Once on a weekend my mom said I could go to a friend's house and hang out for a while. When I was there, my mom went shopping, so when I came home my stepfather was like, "Where have you been?" I was like, "Over at a friend's, Mom said I could go." And then he said, "Well, I didn't tell you you could go, so you can't." So I went in my bedroom and started crying and he comes in and says, "You need to stop crying." And I couldn't and so he just left and said I was "just a real stupid girl, you know, a idiot."

During weekdays when her mother was at home, Kristen had a close and warm relationship with her. As Kristen points out: "My mom taught me everything, like how to tie my shoes, and ride a bike, and how to braid and curl my hair." Kristen reflexively decided to have her hair styled like her mother's hair: "I wanted to be like her because Mom was there, she did it all." Kristen's mother was her major role model and she looked to her for approval. It was at home then where Kristen initially took up a project of femininity as her own and thus constructed a localized and accountable subordinate femininity to her mother's dominating femininity in this setting. Moreover, Kristen reflexively decided to talk with her mother about the stepfather's verbal bullying and her mother assured her she was not a "stupid girl" and to just try to ignore what the stepfather says because it is not true, but also simply "do the best job you can babysitting." Kristen felt reassured and at ease after this conversation with her mother and she reflexively decided not to confront her stepfather, and to attempt to "fill Mom's shoes when she was gone."

However, after the twins were born Kristen also determined that her mother increasingly seemed too busy to interact with her: "She was always like doing laundry, cooking, cleaning, and taking care of the twins. The twins took time away from me being with my mom." Through Kristen's internal deliberations, then, she decided that her mother was spending all of her time with the twins, thus neglecting her, and the twins seemed to be incredibly pampered by her mother:

> They would always get what they wanted. If I was watching something on TV and they wanted to watch something, Mom would always make me change the channel. She just always gave them what they wanted and they got all of Mom's attention.

Kristen thus came to resent this partiality of her mother toward the twins but also she came to accept it as "children take a lot of time."

Arguably then, Kristen identified with her mother, who was her initial model for developing a fundamental feminine project.

And Kristen's interviews clearly showed that within the family a substantial commitment toward, and an at times arduous reproduction of, an accountable subordinate femininity was constructed by Kristen that included numerous localized practices associated with primarily housework and childcare. Indeed, when I asked Kristen what she wanted to be when she grew up, she stated: "I want to be a mommy like my mom!" Although Kristen was subjected to verbal abuse, her mother seemed to help minimize the effects of that victimization, and Kristen never was the victim of, nor did she ever engage in assaultive or sexual violence, in this setting. Nevertheless, throughout junior high school Kristen reflexively discerned a growing detachment in her relationship with her mother, but she reflexively concluded that this was due primarily to her mother's childcare responsibilities.

School Relations

Kristen did reasonably well in elementary and junior high school, and she initially had numerous girlfriends—many of whom she labeled the popular "prep/jocks"—with whom she shared a variety of activities: rollerblading, bicycle riding, playing sports, and going to movies and dances. Kristen was slim at the time, wore what she called "cool-girls' clothes," constructed a dominant femininity, and had never been bullied.

However, approximately halfway through junior high, Kristen reflexively realized she had become extremely overweight: "It was like all of a sudden I saw myself like, wow, I'm really fat. Mostly 'cause my girlfriends told me so." In what seemed to immediately follow her significant weight gain, Kristen became the victim of in-school, constant (every day, throughout the day) verbal and social bullying, primarily from her girlfriends. The bullying concentrated on her physical size and shape (at the time, she was much shorter and much heavier than the other girls), having been labeled "*the* fat girl." As Kristen put it:

> I was now always picked on every day, like, "Oh, here comes the fat girl" or "Oh, look there's the fat girl, the girl with the fat

ass." And then when I walked by they'd just ignore me, make faces at me, and stuff like that, and then just laugh at me. And no one would be my friend anymore. They really changed just because I gained a lot of weight.

Prior to gaining weight, Kristen was also a member of the girls basketball team—"I was point guard"—but now when she attended basketball practice, her dominant feminine friends would verbally bully her during and after each practice: "They would say, 'Oh, *the* fat girl can't dribble' or '*The* fat girl can't shoot—stuff like that.'" And in the school hallways the same dominant girls would say, "You're too fat to play ball" and "You're a fat-ass loser." Following such verbal bullying, the same girls "would just walk away, stare at me, look me up and down, whisper to each other, and then laugh. And they were all of course still slim and pretty and popular, you know." Because of this constant combined verbal and social bullying, Kristen decided to stop playing basketball.

I asked Kristen about the structure of cliques at her school. She mentioned first the "popular kids"—the "jocks" and the "preps" (the "cool" boys and girls, many of whom were members of both groups and represented dominant masculinity and femininity), and second the "unpopular people": the "nerds," the "smart kids," the "chicks" (only girls), the "freaks," the "earthies" (both boys and girls), the "skaters," the "losers," and the "tough guys" (only boys) who represented the subordinate masculinities and femininities. Kristen then discussed how the bullying was related to these cliques:

Q. Which groups are your old girlfriends in?

A. They're both preps and jocks, what I used to be.

Q. You used to be both a prep and a jock?

A. Yeah, before I gained weight.

Q. How does one become a member of both groups?

A. Well, you gotta have a tall, slim body, wear the cool clothes, hang out with the cool guys, and be good at sports. If you do all that, you're what we called the "prep/jock girls."

Q. So the popular girls are also into sports?

A. Well, some sports, like field hockey, basketball, and swimming. But because I gained so much weight I couldn't do sports, so they all called me "*the* fat girl" and "*the* fat-ass loser," and they wouldn't let me be their friend anymore. I was kinda kicked out of both groups, and I felt totally worthless, like I was not important anymore.

Q. Do the prep/jock girls decide who is acceptable and who isn't?

A. Yeah, they decide what is cool to wear and do and stuff. And if you don't do it, go along, you're seen as cheap—you know, worthless.

Q. So they have a lot of power?

A. Oh, yeah. They can like make you or break you, you know. And they decided to break me. I used to be part of them and I liked being in that group; it was fun and they accepted me, so I was never teased. I actually miss being with my old girlfriends 'cause everything was fine then, but now all they do is say mean things to me and totally reject me.

Q. What about the prep/jock boys? How do they treat you?

A. They just like ignore me now. They don't want anything to do with me after I gained weight. And since boys don't like me anymore, my old girlfriends don't either.

Kristin reflexively experienced confusion and anger from the bullying: "At first I was like real angry, you know, because my old girlfriends are so mean to me just for gaining weight. I didn't understand, I was like totally confused." Eventually the anger changed to feelings of sadness, betrayal, and inferiority:

I couldn't believe it was happening, and it just made me more and more sad. I really liked my old girlfriends, and now they didn't want anything to do with me. Like every day I would just go somewhere and cry, all alone. I cried every day for hours because I didn't know what to do. It was like total betrayal, you know. They made me feel like shit, like totally crummy, totally worthless.

I asked Kristen if she talked to anyone about her situation; she said she decided not to mention it to any school officials because "They see it happening all the time and don't do anything about it." She also thought seriously about talking to her stepfather and mother about it, but quickly rejected the former because "He wouldn't care at all—he'd just say I deserved it, something like that, 'cause all he did was tell me how stupid I am. All the time." Kristen decided to approach her mother because "At least she cared a little about me, and I just had to talk to someone." Unfortunately, Kristen's mother did not tell her what she needed to hear:

> She said if someone calls me a name to just walk away, but if someone keeps saying it or hits me, I shouldn't stand there and let them do it: I should hit them for it. She always said that I should hit them if they keep bugging me. But I told her I was afraid to hit them 'cause I'm smaller, like they will beat me up. And she just said that I should just hit 'em, that I don't want them to think they can get away with it. But of course I never did hit them 'cause I'm afraid and I wanted them just to like me. So I never talked to Mom about it again.

Because of the continued feminine subordination through bullying by the dominant prep/jocks, Kristen eventually decided to approach some other girls at school—the "chicks" (a subordinated girl in-school clique)—and "they let me hang out with them." All of the chicks were, likewise, overweight and not involved in sports, but would do all they could to look and act feminine—"I liked that they were into looking real 'hot,' plus I wanted to have friends." The chicks would often go to the local mall after school—and Kristen would tag along—and proceed to shoplift feminine cosmetics and clothes, such as eyeliner, eye shadow, nail polish, and "hot" miniskirts and tight pants. Kristen then decided to begin dressing provocatively like the chicks, and initially she was accepted marginally into the group. But she also noted that her participation as a chick immediately resulted in her old prep/jock girlfriends verbally bullying her by calling her a "slut." Indeed, Kristen's old girlfriends now daily bullied her not only for her size and shape but also because of her changed attire and practice: "The prep/jocks always teased us chicks, especially me, and make fun of us for the way we dress and act." According to her old girlfriends, the chicks (including Kristen) who daily dressed in "short jean miniskirts with black tights," or "tight little flares, heels, tank tops, lots a makeup, curled hair, and brightly painted finger nails," and who acted in "a sexy way"—such as "walk past some guys real slow, swinging our ass, and then look back at them with a big smile"—were simply "fat sluts." In fact, Kristen stated that the prep/jocks often called her this name because she did not dress and act a certain way; for example, "The prep/jocks called me a 'fat slut' because they said I tried to look pretty, but I was to them just a 'makeup-covered fat-ass slut'—that's the way they put it." One of the prep/jocks—who was Kristen's best friend when she was a member of that group—actually told her that she looked "like a 'sleazy whore' who should be out on the street rather than at school." After asking Kristen to describe how the dominant "prep/jock" girls were different from the subordinated "chicks," she stated:

> They don't wear as much makeup and stuff, and not the same type of clothes, but they're tall and slim and pretty but do their hair different, and the guys come to them, you know; they have their pick of guys, and they all have a boyfriend. The chicks don't really have boyfriends, they just kinda romance guys, you know, date guys, go after them, and the prep/jocks don't like that.

When the "chicks" were verbally bullied as "slut" for presenting differently from the "prep/jock" girls, they would, according to Kristen, often respond by shouting "just shut up," and then they would call the prep/jocks "skinny sticks" and "anorexic bulimic snobs." Consequently, for a short time Kristen felt solidarity with the chicks, and her membership in this group helped alleviate the feelings of distress and inadequacy produced by the dominant prep/jock bullying: "Being a chick helped me a lot 'cause now I didn't feel alone, you know, and I kinda liked being a hot chick, you know, and I didn't feel like I needed my old girlfriends anymore."

Nonetheless, the bullying by the dominant prep/jocks continued unabated, and in due course Kristen became the subject of serious verbal bullying by the chicks as well. Kristen put it this way: "They [the chicks] would always like be talking about sex and stuff, like giving blow jobs and hand jobs, you know, and like even two chicks bragged about having babies." And it was during her participation in the chicks group—and her strong desire to be what she called "a hot chick"—that she became much more interested in heterosexuality: Kristen reflexively decided she wanted to experience sexuality with boys and "learn what it was like and what it was all about." Thus it was in the "chick" setting that Kristen began to attach a more intensified heterosexual project to her femininity. Although Kristen attempted to attract boys sexually—"I really wanted to have sex with some of the guys at school, so I would go up to them and like try to talk to them"—the boys uniformly rejected her offerings, one stating bluntly that he was not interested in a "slutty fat ass." Consequently, Kristen described herself as "still a virgin" and, therefore, unable to share in the "sex talk" with the other chicks. Indeed, when the chicks found out she was a virgin, "They started calling me the 'peewee virgin' like all the time and started acting like it's a requirement to have sex, you know, to be a chick. And some just ignored me, walked away when I tried to talk to them, made me feel like totally unwanted." Thus Kristen now constructed a subordinate femininity within the chick group as well.

Kristen reported that internally she felt "totally embarrassed" by this new subordinating development because she really wanted to be accepted as a chick: "I wanted to do stuff the way the chicks do it." However, Kristen reflexively realized that because she was a "virgin" she did not qualify, once again feeling shame and inadequacy for her inability to become a *real* chick. Kristen's feelings of sadness and inferiority returned, and indeed intensified. With no one to talk to about her distressing situation, Kristen increasingly felt powerless and a total lack of control over her life: "I really wanted to be a chick, you know. But they wouldn't let me. I didn't fit in anywhere 'cause everybody rejected me. My old girlfriends rejected me and the chicks rejected me. I was really sad. It was really hard. I had no idea what to do."

Because of the constant bullying victimization from both the prep/jocks and the chicks—and her resulting insecurity—Kristen developed an intense fear of school: "I was afraid to go to school because it seemed like everyone hated me—I didn't measure up to anyone. It was like I didn't have any friends, no one to call my friend. I was totally lonely, like all alone all the time. I really wanted to be like the other girls but couldn't."

Sexual Violence at the Park

By age fourteen, Kristen was experiencing severe bullying victimization at school by both the dominant prep/jocks—over her physical size and shape, her alleged "slutty" presentation, and her inability to participate in sports—and by the subordinate chicks for being a "peewee virgin." Kristen's reflexively identified serious lack of feminine resources created a negative feminine self-esteem—she felt inadequate as a "girl"—and her feminine insecurity was aggravated further by her inability to become a real "hot chick" through primarily developing sexual relationships with boys her age. Consequently, Kristen reflexively concluded that she was completely powerless in relation to the prep/jocks and the chicks.

Then one day, during her eighth-grade year in junior high, Kristen was "hanging out" at a park playground near her home where she came upon a seven-year-old boy sitting on the grass next to the merry-go-round. (At this time Kristen was experiencing the unbearable distressing events just discussed and was simultaneously at the juncture where she "discovered" heterosexuality through participation in the chick group.) Kristen approached the boy and sat next to him: "And all I could think about is that I want to have sex like the chicks. No guys at school liked me and so I thought, hey, maybe I can do it with this boy, you know." I then asked Kristen to describe what happened next:

> Well, I was like a lot bigger than him and he seemed kinda shy, you know. And I just thought that I'm bigger than him and so I could just get him to do it.
>
> Q. So what did you do? Did you force him?

A. Not really force him. Like no one was around, we're the only ones in the park, and I just told him how cute he was and that he had real cool clothes, you know, stuff like that.

Q. Why did you say these things to him?

A. I just wanted him to be okay with me, you know, not be scared.

Kristen went on to explain that after a short time they were lying together on the park grass in a very secluded area, looking up at the sky and talking about the shape of the clouds and "he was having a real good time." The boy seemed to enjoy Kristen's company, and then at what Kristen defined as "the best time" she reflexively decided to sit up "and I just like opened his pants, and started to like real easy rub and feel his penis." According to Kristen, "He just kept lying on the grass and closed his eyes. It was like he just really liked it. He didn't say anything or fight me, so I just kept doing it." After approximately five minutes, Kristen decided to close his pants and she asked him if he would be at the park playground the next day, "and he said yes!" I then asked Kristen if they met at the playground the next day and she replied: "Yep, and we did the same thing and he actually got kinda aroused and so did I. He enjoyed it and I did too. I used my hand in a nice way, you know, and then we met again at the park the next day, and we did the same thing." The following dialogue reveals what the sexual offending accomplished for Kristen:

Q. Why did you do this?

A. I wanted to try sex, you know, 'cause all the prep/jocks and chicks bragged about doing it. It was a cool thing to do and I thought I should do it too. And I couldn't do it the way they did so I did it this way.

Q. How did it make you feel to do this?

A. When I was doing it I felt real good, like he might actually like me doing it, you know. He seemed to like it and I liked that. And I like decided what to do, and that felt good, you know, 'cause I never had that either.

I then asked Kristen to expand on the notions of "feeling good" and "decided what to do" when she engaged in these sexual offenses, and she stated:

I mean it felt good I could pretty much do anything I want with him, even open his pants and feel him, you know. I didn't want to hurt him at all and I didn't, but it was such a turn on 'cause I could just like do whatever I wanted, you know. He never complained or said anything to me, he was just like real quiet. And so I was like, wow, I'm doing whatever I want, and he's not saying anything, not giving me any shit, not saying anything bad to me, not being mean or anything to me.

Kristen went on to point out that the sexual offending also "felt good" because "this is like cool, you know, 'cause I felt like a chick now"—from Kristen's point of view, she was now practicing dominant chick heterofemininity. And Kristen reflexively determined that her power and control over this boy was somewhat similar to that of the prep/jock and chick girls:

You know these girls are so looked up to and it was like this boy looked up to me. But I couldn't tell anyone, you know, but I still liked it 'cause it's like something I should have, 'cause the preps and chicks had it, you know, people looking up to them. And it felt good to be kinda like them. You know what I mean?

Q. I think I know what you mean. It made you feel like a "hot chick" who is now sexual and people like you looked up to them. Is that right?

A. Yeah, kinda, 'cause at school I didn't really feel like a hot chick 'cause they said I wasn't really, and no guys were gonna have sex with me, you know. But when I rubbed his penis I kinda felt like them, you know, 'cause I'm doing what they brag about, and people looked up to them for that. And the preps and chicks were strong and could do stuff, and nobody say anything back 'cause they looked up to them. And I couldn't do that at school, but I could do that with this boy, you know. So, yeah, it was kinda like that, and I liked it.

Q. Why did you choose this boy and not a girl—it was girls who mostly bullied you, right?

A. No way would I choose a girl, I'm not that way. I'm straight all the way, so I wouldn't.

Kristen continued on this topic of object choice by stating that the sexual offenses had nothing to do with revenge, as it was not intended to "get back" at the girls who bullied her. Rather, the primary reflexive motive was to "try sex," and that the power and control over the boy during the assaults was unexpectedly an added bonus. Despite "feeling good" during sexual offending, soon after the third offense, the boy told his parents everything and Kristen seemed surprised at this development: "I never thought he would 'cause he didn't seem to mind. I never hurt him or even tried to scare him at all. It was like I didn't need too. That just never entered my mind, but he did tell on me."

Gender Conformity and Nonviolence at Home

What do these two life stories teach us about the relationship among sex, gender, sexuality, and nonviolence in the home setting? For Sam, he confronted the constraints and possibilities established through patriarchal gender relations at home and his active adoption of certain forms of social action. Primarily bonding with his father, the two often worked together with tools and went fishing and hunting. Along with Sam's daily chores, the above activities were his major gender practices at home. Accordingly, Sam embodied a subordinate masculinity in relation to his father's dominating masculinity and he oriented his actions for his father's approval—it meant "a lot" to Sam when his father mentioned that he did a "good job helping him." Thus, Sam's subordinate masculinity seemingly was never challenged in this milieu by father or by others. Sam was accountably masculine at home as he engaged in situationally normative masculine conduct that aligned with his male appearance, and such embodied masculinity helped reproduce in-home gender relations; sexuality was essentially insignificant and therefore was not salient to Sam's sense of self in the in-home setting. Distancing himself from the feminine practices of his mother and

sister—except when helping with household cleaning tasks—
Sam confidently, and for the most part unreflexively, embodied
a masculine presence and *place* at home; he was a nonviolent
gender conformist in this setting.

Kristen likewise confronted the constraints and possibilities established through patriarchal gender relations at home,
and she actively adopted specific types of feminine practices.
Kristen's embodied social action at home articulated primarily
with those of her mother—Kristen wants to be like her mother
because she "does it all"—and thus Kristen constructed a subordinate femininity in relation to her mother's dominating
femininity. The available salient practices at home that Kristen
primarily engaged in centered on housework and childcare; to
be sure, through interaction with her mother, Kristen developed a budding feminine project in this setting: "I want to be a
mommy like Mom"—and Kristen therefore accountably embodied a localized nonviolent subordinate femininity through her
female appearance and gender practices.

After her twin sisters were born, Kristen's mother often
would depart from the home for lengthy time periods, thereby
leaving Kristen alone with her stepfather and sisters. Increasingly the stepfather would demand that Kristen babysit her
sisters—thus relieving him of this responsibility—and if she did
anything wrong in the process he would verbally abuse her.
Thus, on the occasions when her mother was absent from the
home, Kristen transformed into a "surrogate wife" who, under
conditions of constant femininity challenges from her stepfather,
practiced emphasized femininity in relation to his hegemonic
masculinity. Taking the advice of her mother to simply "ignore"
his verbal bullying and "do the best job you can," Kristen thus
engaged once again in situationally normative feminine conduct
(in this situation "emphasized femininity") that aligned with
her feminine appearance, and such embodied femininity helped
reproduce in-home patriarchal gender relations; Kristen became
an accountable "surrogate wife" in this setting. Nevertheless,
within the overall "site" of the home, sexuality for Kristen was
only salient in the sense of her realization that women become
mommies by producing children.

Repression, Reflexivity, and Recognition

Both Sam and Kristen grew up in homes whereby they were regarded as "gender conformists" and neither personally experienced assaultive or sexual violence nor did they engage in any form of violence against family members in this setting. In contrast, within the setting of the school, like Lenny and Kelly, a social process developed involving repression, reflexivity, and recognition that resulted in both being designated "gender deviants" and subsequently engaging in sexual violence. Let me briefly outline this social process and thus pathway to sexual violence.

Repression

Like Lenny and Kelly in chapter 3, both Sam and Kristen experienced peer interaction in the social setting of the school that oppressively accentuated a very specific type of verbal and social bullying that centered on the body and featured a perceived imbalance between sex category and gender behavior. What these interview data show is that the meaning assigned by the in-school dominant bullies to Sam's and Kristen's *gender behavior* is influenced through their *perceived sex category*. In other words, like Lenny and Kelly in chapter 3, for both Sam and Kristen, because their sex category was judged to be incongruent with their gender behavior, they subsequently became victims of gender repression through consistent bullying.

For Sam, there was an imbalance between his perceived male category and his alleged unmanly behavior and body (e.g., he did not physically "fight back" when bullied and he had a nonmuscular "fat" and "wimpish" body). In other words, Sam's alleged feminine body size/shape and bodily behavior were viewed by the in-school dominant bullies as controverting his perceived (male) sex category. According to the dominant bullies, then, Sam simply was a "wimp" and a "mama's boy" who therefore "failed" to accomplish dominant masculinity in terms of appropriate bodily display and practice. Yet, because he was identified as a "male," he was consistently defined as a "gender deviant" and repressed through bullying victimization.

For Kristen, there was a disparity between her identified female-sex category and her alleged "unwomanly" body and behavior: According to the in-school dominant bullies, she had a "fat" and thereby "unfeminine" body, and that same body simultaneously did not participate in sports. Moreover, like Kelly in chapter 3, we clearly detect the intersection of gender and sexuality: according to the same bullies, Kristen eventually was labeled a "fat-ass slut," and according to the chicks, Kristen simply was a "peewee virgin." Thus, the subordinated sexual terms of "slut" and "virgin"—at opposite ends of the teenage-girl heterosexual spectrum—are assigned to Kristen for not displaying and practicing "proper" heterofemininity. Kristen's body size and shape and her bodily display and behavior then were viewed by both the dominant prep/jock and chick bullies as controverting her female-sex category. Thus, Kristen "failed," according to the bullies, to accomplish situationally dominant heterofemininity in terms of appropriate bodily display and practice; yet, because she was identified as a "female," she was consistently defined as a "heterofeminine deviant" and repressed through consistent bullying.

For Sam and Kristen, then, their bodies and their bodily display/behavior conveyed a sex/gender—and sexuality for Kristen—combined image at school that the bullies viewed as a misalignment between sex category and gender/sexual display/behavior—this clearly was a different interaction than both experienced at home. And it was this situationally recognized bodily imbalance by the bullies and their attempt at repression—as conveyed through their verbal and social bullying—that *motivated* Sam and Kristen to engage in reflexivity, to which we now turn.

Reflexivity

Through reflexivity both Sam and Kristen realized initially that their bodies *restrained* their gender *and* sexual agency: Sam could not embody the in-school dominant-boy expectations—he had a "fat" and "wimpish" body and he was unable to achieve heterosexual masculine expectations; Kristen could not embody the in-school girl expectations—she no longer presented a slim body, she was not successful in attracting "cool guys," she was labeled a "slut" *and* a "virgin," and she was unfit to participate in sports. Further reflexivity led Sam and Kristen to attempt specific practices to solve and/or minimize their individual dilemma—Sam and Kristen talked with their father and mother respectively who suggested, likewise, to physically fight back. However, Sam and Kristen quickly dismissed this "advice" as an impossible option given the size and shape of their bodies. Like Lenny and Kelly, then, both Sam's and Kristen's bodies actually were participating in their reflexive agency by limiting available, and suggesting possible, courses of social action. Sam and Kristen wanted to stop the bullying, yet they realized through reflexivity the limits of their embodied action: initially they could not retaliate physically against the bullies; thus their bodies restrained their agency. Consequently, Sam and Kristen attempted to salvage some type of control over the situation through different reflexive embodied social action: Sam internally decided to become a loner at school; Kristen internally decided to physically escape to a safe space and to cry. However, these specific reflexive social actions failed to solve, much less improve, the oppressive situation. In fact, the bullying by the dominant boys and girls against Sam and Kristen relentlessly continued.

During reflexivity, then, both Sam and Kristen came to internally conceptualize themselves in the way that others perceived them—they reified the images communicated by others. Much of this internal conceptualization was arrived at by way of interaction and communication with others. Through such interaction and communication, both Sam and Kristen took an "external" view of themselves, thus becoming the objects of their own reflexivity. Because of the shame and mortification resulting from persistent daily repression through bullying victimization, the assault upon Sam's and Kristen's self-definition and social identification intensified. This assault drove both to move from a taken-for-granted relationship with their bodies to a more enhanced reflexive one. In other words, they intensely internalized the "external" by engaging in reflexivity; in the process, they both, through internal conversations, determined their courses of action in relation to their bodies and their social circumstances.

However, Kristen engaged in a practice clearly unavailable to Sam. Unable to embody dominant prep/jock femininity, yet simultaneously in extreme need of friendship and feminine accomplishment, Kristen reflexively decided to seek acceptance as a member of a different subordinate group of girls who she assumed would be empathetic. Consequently, her body once again became an agent of her reflexive social action: Kristen discovered a girl's group with similar feminine bodily presentations—she sought to become a "hot chick" among similarly overweight girls who were uninterested in sports. Unfortunately, her efforts to curb the bullying by developing these new female friendships met with much misfortune, as the bullying victimization actually escalated. Kristen now embodied two subordinate feminine identities: from the prep/jocks, Kristen was no longer simply *"the* fat girl," she was now a "fat-ass *slut*"; and from the chicks, she acquired the identity of "peewee *virgin*." Thus, for Kristen her internal feelings of distress and powerlessness worsened because of her unsuccessful attempt to be accepted by *any* of her male and female peers.

Although Sam was not similarly bullied in terms of sexuality, he did observe the in-school dominant "cool guys" sexualizing girls as objects of heterosexual desire and actually realizing such heterosexual expectations. Not surprisingly, Sam reflexively and similarly objectified girls and internally determined that he also wanted to participate in the same sexual practices but he was unable to achieve such masculine expectations. Like Kristen in relation to the dominant preps/jocks and chicks, Sam found his own sexuality through observation of the dominant males at school, and engaging in heterosexuality became for him an important reflexive resource for doing heteromasculinity; yet Sam was unable to accomplish such practices at school. Differing from Lenny and Kelly, then, for Sam and Kristen heterosexuality became extraordinarily *salient* in the in-school social setting. And Sam's reflexive feelings of distress and powerlessness, like Kristen's, intensified because of an inability to be accepted by *any* of his male or female peers.

In short, Sam and Kristen found themselves internally deliberating about their individual social circumstances—which clearly were significantly different from their interactions at home—and, in particular, they intensely engaged in reflexivity, reflecting on their body to determine what they could and could not "do" to overcome their subordinating social situations. Accordingly, their bodies became reflexive participants in the generating and shaping of their social practices.

Recognition

Extending their reflexivity into further social action, the control, power, and "sexuality" associated with sexual manipulation, exploitation, and domination of the girls by Sam and the boy by Kristen provided each with a contextually based heteromasculine and heterofeminine respective resource when other such resources were unavailable. For Sam and Kristen, the sexual assaults established situations whereby they now reflexively embodied heteromasculinity/femininity—from their point of view they invalidated any definition of themselves as a "heterogender deviant" and they had complete control over another person or persons. Given the private nature of their sexual offending, however, Sam and Kristen were subjected continually to derogatory verbal bullying at school, all of which reinforced their feelings of heteromasculine/feminine inadequacy. Indeed, their bodies continued to restrain their heterogender agency in the public-school arena, and therefore their consistent achievement exclusively of this private form of heteromasculinity/femininity through the serial sexual assaults, at least until their violence was revealed.

Reflecting upon their own bodies in relation to the bodies of the children they sexually assaulted, Sam's and Kristen's bodies became agents of their social action: they came to situationally facilitate heteromasculine/feminine agency and to validate some type of private masculine/feminine sexual self, an agency that constructed certain gender and sexual ways of interacting with and through their bodies. Indeed, both Sam and Kristen viewed dominant masculinity/femininity—through interaction at school—as in part a synthesizing of male/female sex category with heteromasculinity/femininity (practiced through specific gender and heterosexual practices) and with the power to control others without the fear of retaliation (bullying). The private sexual offending allowed Sam and Kristen to accomplish these gender and sexual demands, as their "sex" now seemingly aligned with their "heterogender."

Both Sam and Kristen were disallowed participation in any type of heteromasculinity/femininity in the social setting of the school. Consequently, the behavioral expressions activated by such contextual gender and sexual challenges could be directed only outside the school setting. In this sense, then, the bodies of Sam and Kristen became party to a surrogate heteromasculine/feminine practice that directed them toward a course of social action that was bodily realizable. Sam and Kristen had a desperate need to abandon their subordinate position and to fit into some type of acceptable heteromasculinity/femininity offered at school—a particular heterosexual imperative was intertwined with each of their understandings of acceptable masculinity and femininity. For Sam and Kristen, then, the heteromasculinity/femininity practiced at school was not rejected. Rather, gender and heterosexual subordination directed Sam and Kristen toward reflexively fixating on specific sites (the home and a park playground) and a specific form of body deployment (sexual offending) where such practices—and thus a balance between sex appearance and gender/sexual behavior—could be realized. Moreover, both Sam and Kristen had access to less-powerful children in these settings and, therefore, had the means through which their bodies could attain some type of heteromasculine/feminine expression. Indeed, the contrast, primarily in age and body size, created a power differential that ultimately was agentic for both Sam and Kristen but offensive to the child victims who were physically, mentally, and socially weaker. Given that Sam and Kristen were removed from any type of recognized heteromasculine/feminine status in any adolescent in-school milieu, the available "sexual" opportunity at the above sites were especially attractive, became obsessive, and provided a powerful and exclusive means of doing heteromasculinity/femininity.

In attempting to masculinize/feminize and heterosexualize their bodies within the fascinating and absorbing conceptualization of in-school dominant heteromasculinity/femininity, Sam and Kristen engendered a specific heteromasculine/feminine sense of self through manipulative and exploitative sexual offending against young children. It was in the "sites" of the home and the park that Sam's and Kristen's bodies took on a relatively new size and shape (both are physically larger and stronger than their victims) and that their bodies moved in a different way than at school (both were physically bold, competent, and dominant in the home/park settings). By concentrating their interactional efforts outside the context of the school, Sam and Kristen—like Lenny and Kelly—were able now to transform how they interacted with and through their bodies; from their point of view, their sex appearance and gender behavior were now aligned as they validated their "sex" through "heterosexuality." Both Sam and Kristen were now living through their bodies in a new way and thus they became, in their own eyes, gender and sexual conformists. The reflexive choice to engage in sexual offending, then, was a situational resource through which Sam and Kristen could be heteromasculine/feminine through bodily practice, temporarily resolving their unremitting struggle for heteromasculine/feminine *recognition*.

I will have more to say about Sam and Kristen in chapter 6. Before that, however, in the following chapter I present two nonviolent life histories.

5

Nonviolence
Jerry and Karen

Chapter 5 focuses on a white working-class boy and girl involved in nonviolence: Jerry and Karen (both pseudonyms). Jerry and Karen were chosen specifically from the larger pool of interviewees for three explicit reasons. First, both Jerry and Karen grew up in homes whereby neither personally experienced assaultive or sexual violence. Thus, these two case studies are consistent with those in chapters 3 and 4 in that they facilitate comparison of all six boys and girls who grew up in a home setting in which they were not physically or sexually victimized nor did they engage in assaultive or sexual violence against family members. Second, Karen did not admit committing a violent act nor had she been formally charged with committing a violent offense at the time of the interviews; Jerry admitted engaging in violence (but had never been formally charged) for a brief period early in his life (at a young age) and thereafter adopted an exclusively nonviolent pattern of behavior. Thus these two case studies enable comparison of a girl who had never been violent with a boy who initially was violent but then became exclusively nonviolent. Finally, the two case studies are nicely juxtaposed because both Karen and Jerry grew up in the same neighborhood and attended the same school at the same time. Accordingly, this chapter reports data as to why a boy and a girl from the *same* social milieu engaged in nonviolence for both similar and different reasons. We begin this chapter with Jerry.

Jerry

Jerry was a tall, slightly overweight seventeen-year-old who displayed considerable maturity and self-reliance. He had short dark hair, a plump, cute face, and he wore a button-down long-sleeve shirt, baggy jeans, and tennis shoes to both interviews. Jerry presented the relaxed deportment of a happy and at-ease individual who engaged easily in conversation with an adult; we seemingly could have discussed his life for days. In what follows, I describe, through Jerry's words, his family relations at home and his eventual nonviolence at home, school, and on the street.

Family Relations

Jerry lives in a small house located in the center of a working-class town. His earliest memory is living alone with his mother, who had separated from his father because of his alcohol abuse. To make ends meet, Jerry's mother worked two jobs in the un-skilled-labor market. Early on Jerry felt very close to his mother. Although she worked a lot, he was proud of the fact that "she managed to keep things together for us."

While his mother worked, Jerry was cared for by several different couples who were friends of the family. Depending on the day of the week and the time of day, Jerry would stay with one or another of the couples. Although he rotated among "babysitting" families, he has only fond memories of the many adults who cared for him: "They were all great. I had a lot of fun with all of them."

Around the age of six Jerry met his biological father for the first time. He explained to me how this meeting emerged:

> I had always asked, "Hey, where is Dad?" 'cause I always saw these kids with their dad. My mom is always really honest

with me. That's the way we've always been, really straightforward with each other. She told me that he was a recovering alcoholic and that maybe someday I'd see him. Finally she called my grandfather and found out where my dad was, and called him, and they set up a thing where he came over to the house.

Jerry thought it was "really cool" when he first met his father because they had a wonderful time together; they went for a walk in the park and spent the entire afternoon side by side as one. Before Jerry's father left that day "we made plans to get back together soon." And it was not long after this first meeting with his father that Jerry's parents actually reconciled and all three began living under the same roof. This was exciting to Jerry because now he was like the other kids—he had both a mother and a father, and he loved his father immensely.

Jerry's father owned a small business in the unskilled manual-labor market and "worked very hard at it." He worked full-time during the day and was extremely tired when he came home in the afternoon. Nevertheless, "we'd play games and watch TV and stuff like that. He'd take me places and we'd just hang out together." When I asked Jerry who his heroes were when he was in elementary school, he stated:

My dad for one of them because he did really hard work and everything. So that made me pretty proud of him. I always respected people that did hard work—my grandfather, great grandfather, those kinds of folks.

Q. What was it about hard work that impressed you?

A. Well, when you've finished hard work it really shows that you have done something.

Q. Did that have a masculine image to you?

A. Not really, because my mom worked hard at two jobs and I knew she was working hard to keep the family up.

Q. What did you want to be when you grew up?

A. I wanted to be like my dad and mom: a hard worker at something I liked to do.

This closeness, with his father in particular, nourished Jerry's idea of future labor-force participation: Jerry wants to have a similar business after finishing high school and work hard at it. "If I start my business right out of school and I do it smart, by learning from Dad's mistakes that he's made, I can go on to have a wicked business."

Jerry was also extremely pleased and proud that his father overcame addiction to alcohol. The two were so close that Jerry would attend the "alcohol rehab" meetings with his father, and then the two would talk after the meeting. Jerry has affectionate memories not only of his father speaking up at the meetings but also of the special talks afterward. In particular, his father always expressed to Jerry during these conversations that it was not Jerry's fault that he became an alcoholic—Jerry's father took full responsibility for his addiction. Because Jerry's father was contributing economically to the household, his mother was able to quit one of her two jobs and had time to pursue other interests (e.g., she enrolled part-time at a local university, where she took classes now and then based on personal interests).

Despite these positive developments, Jerry's parents seemed unable to get along with each other. Their difficulties were not related to his father's past problems with alcohol—he remained alcohol-free—or his mother's attending university. Rather, their problems centered on financial issues and consisted of verbal battles—never any physical violence—between the two. Jerry discussed with both parents the issues involved and the nature of the arguments; they consistently stated that the arguments were not Jerry's fault but only reflected an inability to work out financial matters. "There never was anything negative towards me from my parents, always positive things." Although these arguments were among the most distressing events in Jerry's family life, his parents always protected Jerry from responsibility for their problems. In fact, Jerry and his parents were very "connected." Jerry experienced a warm and affectionate relationship with both. "We did everything together. We'd go cross-country skiing, we'd go camping, go on hikes—we were quite an outdoor family." Jerry went hunting and fishing with his dad, helped his mom and dad in the kitchen, and helped his mom in the garden. "I always liked being in the kitchen" and "there was this wonderful garden that me and my mom would be in together."

When Jerry was in elementary school and junior high school, he was responsible for some of the household chores, such as emptying the garbage, getting wood, feeding the pets, setting the table, cutting the lawn, and helping with the cooking and cleaning. Both parents worked together to cook the evening meal. Jerry remembers especially that sometimes "I'd get home from school and I could smell just-baked pies as I walked up the driveway. There would like be three pies on the table that my dad baked. And I'd be like, oh yeah!" Although his father worked at a "masculine" job and his mother at a "feminine" job, at home Jerry observed and participated in both "masculine" and "feminine" forms of domestic labor. Nevertheless, Jerry never particularly liked chores, and frequently performed them in a "real half-ass way." Although his parents would be upset with him for his performance of these duties, he was never disciplined harshly. "They would never send me to my room or anything like that. They'd take stuff away, you know, like no radio in my room. Or they'd threaten me that I couldn't do certain stuff on weekends." Jerry was never spanked by either parent. Although he clearly identified with his father, Jerry's mother also had a major influence on him. His parents' participation in household labor—as well as their renunciation of interpersonal physical violence—defined for him an alternative form of masculinity that differed from the hegemonic models practiced by fathers/stepfathers in the households discussed in chapters 3 and 4. Indeed, Jerry's father and mother respectively embodied a localized equality masculinity and femininity and Jerry seemed to adopt what was offered—it is in this setting that Jerry began to take up a project of this type of masculinity as his own; his fundamental gender project was to be like "Dad." Thus, Jerry embodied an accountably nonviolent equality masculinity through both his sex appearance and his gender practices at home.

Violence at School

For Jerry, school was not as congenial a place as home. He was an average student and from elementary school on through high school Jerry was the target of consistent verbal bullying for being overweight. "I was called 'chubby' and 'fat ass' a lot. I was laughed at, pushed around, and it would really drag me down." Indeed, because of the comments from kids at school Jerry reflexively did not like to go to school or to be seen in public because he accepted the way others characterized his body. "I didn't like going out in public because I felt small and insecure. I was average height but fat. I did a lot of stuff by myself and didn't go out a lot."

> Q. You were very concerned about the way you looked?
>
> A. Well, as a kid you're always concerned about your physical looks. And I was very concerned about how people saw me and the way I saw myself.
>
> Q. Can you expand on that a little for me?
>
> A. Oh, just really low self-esteem, just a bad self-image of myself. I didn't like myself if that's the way other people saw me. I was big outside but I felt small inside.

As a result of verbal bullying and acute distress over his body, Jerry developed a painful lack of masculine self-esteem at school. Consequently, in third grade he reflexively decided to become involved in a number of "fistfights." These fights were simply part of what Jerry labeled "playground business," which he defined as "some kid does something and the other kid takes it as he has insulted him, so he goes up and hits the kid for insulting him. That's how kids in my grade school handled business on the playground." Being teased and bullied made Jerry internally feel subordinate, insecure, and small. So during his internal deliberations about this he decided he would respond according to the playground definition of appropriately handling such "business." "Kids would bully me and then I'd feel better by bullying other kids. If I got bullied, then I had to put someone down by beating the shit out of him." If Jerry did not bully or fight back, he would be called a wimp: "Kids would keep bullying me." Jerry reflexively decided that he wanted to be "tough" in front of the other kids, so he got into eight fights that year. The following dialogue further develops this topic:

> Q. Did you fight back against the kids who bullied you?
>
> A. Yeah, sometimes, and sometimes I'd go after other kids.

Q. How did that make you feel?

A. It made me feel that if I could bring somebody else down, then I would be higher than them and that was better.

Q. You beat up some kids?

A. Oh, yeah. I lost some and won some.

Like Lenny and Sam, then, the verbal bullying constructed a gender challenge for Jerry, as he was now defined as subordinate and feminine and thus the dominant bullies-Jerry relationship actually was a momentary hegemonic masculinity in the making—and Jerry reflexively decided to respond in a way that the culture of the school emphasized, that is, with physical violence, which somewhat minimized that feminization.

School, Street, and Nonviolence

I asked Jerry if he discussed this bullying and fighting with either parent, and he said "of course." In fact, all three—Mom, Dad, and Jerry—discussed the issue together after his first fight: "They sat me down and had a nice talk with me. They were like, 'Oh, we're really sorry,' and they told me it wasn't my fault when I was bullied and everything, and just to next time turn my back. Not to fight."

Q. Your parents didn't tell you to bully back or fight back?

A. No, my mom and dad never said that. My mom is against that, you know, the macho thing about guys that have to puff themselves all up and everything.

Q. Did your parents teach you to handle these kinds of problems in a nonviolent way?

A. Yeah. My mom wanted me to see that you didn't have to do that and my dad is the same way. We talked about it quite a bit. My parents would say, "It's the other kid's problem. There's something wrong with kids that bully kids."

At first Jerry reflexively decided not to accept his parents' suggestion and he reflexively decided to continue to respond in a physically violent way at school. Jerry explained that he felt he could not simply "walk away" because "you have to show kids you're not afraid to do it. My mom and dad didn't understand what it was like." The following extended dialogue demonstrates how eventually Jerry reflexively accepted a nonviolent response to these challenges at school:

Q. But after each fight you talked to your parents about it?

A. Oh, yeah. We've always had a very open relationship.

Q. Both parents were telling you to just walk away, but at the same time you felt you could not because you had to show other kids that you were tough?

A. Right. My mom and dad said [to] walk away and the kids on the playground said show that you are tough. It was very confusing for a little kid.

Q. How did you resolve this dilemma?

A. My mom and dad had more and more of these talks with me, and around the fifth grade what they were saying began to sink in.

Q. It was the persistence of your parents then that changed your mind?

A. Yeah, and I did kind of experiments at school where if a kid started saying stuff I would just walk away. And that's when it really started to sink in. It was nice, and I'd come home and say to my parents, "Hey, you guys are right."

Q. When you walked away didn't the kids continue to bully and tease you?

A. Yeah, but I could deal with it because I knew that I wasn't going to get into trouble. Knowing that if they get caught telling me I'm a "wimp" and "fat ass" that they are going to be the ones in trouble. That felt good.

Q. But how did you deal with the idea that you might still be a wimp because you didn't fight back?

A. It was the talks with my parents. They'd reassure me that you were stronger to walk away than to put up your dukes

and fight about it. And then I did that and I started to understand that "hey, they're right and it works."

Jerry indicated that his parents' emphasis on solving interpersonal problems in a nonviolent manner probably had
something to do with the fact that his mother had subscribed to
Ms. magazine and was "into the whole feminist thing." While
attending part-time classes, Jerry's mother met a number of
women and began to participate in a feminist support group.
"There's like four or five women that she sees once or twice a
month."

Q. Did your mother introduce you to some feminist ideas?

A. A couple of things 'cause she was taking women's studies
classes.

Q. Did your mother teach you about how to handle the bullying?

A. Yeah. She'd be like, "Just brush it off." So that's how I kind
of have gotten around it. It's just brushing it off. You know, I
would say to myself, "There must be something wrong with
this kid if they feel they have to make fun of me."

Q. So it was interaction with your mother that convinced you
not to fight back when bullied?

A. Right. But Dad and Mom never encouraged fighting. I
learned from them that if I was picked on I should find a different way to respond. Both Mom and Dad said that.

Despite the fact that Jerry continued to be the victim of bullying, these discussions with his parents convinced him to never
again respond by fighting. Instead, he reflexively decided to
simply walk away. "Usually it resolves itself. You just walk away
and the kid doesn't even say anything to you because he can't get
a rise out of you." Jerry reflexively concluded that this is the best
way to handle such a situation. Thus, although Jerry continued
to be defined as subordinate in relation to the dominant masculine boys at school, he now felt confident responding this way
because, although the bully continues "as you're walking away,

later it's like you just don't even acknowledge that he's there." Consequently, Jerry successfully opposed in-school dominant and hegemonic masculinities through his construction of a form of equality masculinity.

Jerry first learned about sexuality in seventh grade. "I was snooping around the house one day and I found that my parents had the *Joy of Sex* books, and so I looked at them a lot." He also heard from kids at school about heterosexuality. "Guys would talk about it all the time—having sex and stuff with girls." Thus, it was a combination of both home and school interaction that led Jerry to take up a heterosexual project and attach it to his masculinity. And he had two girlfriends in junior high school, one in seventh grade, and one in eighth grade; neither friendship progressed beyond "going out on dates." Jerry eventually decided to mention the books to his parents and several times they looked through them together. On one occasion Jerry and his parents were scanning through the books when they "came to these two girls that were having sex and I was like, 'What's this?'" Jerry's parents explained that the women were lesbians and that "some people were into that kind of thing." When they told him that his sexual orientation was "up to him," he told his parents that he "always liked the female body." He also learned at this time that his two older cousins were gay. Jerry said that he and his mother frequently had tea with several gay and lesbian friends. In any event, there was arguably no "emphasis"—simply "balance"—and it is here that Jerry began to construct an equality heteromasculine project as his own.

Although successful in teaching Jerry how to handle interpersonal problems at school in a nonconflictual way, his parents continued to disagree over family finances. Indeed, these disagreements escalated to the point where they decided that divorce was the only option. Consequently, when Jerry was in the sixth grade his father moved out of the house. Jerry was extremely sad about the divorce but, as he put it, "There was still love and affection from both of them. It just wasn't at the same time." He continued to spend considerable time with both parents on a regular basis. "They'd always say, 'We're having our own problems and it's not your fault.'" Jerry never felt he was the cause of the divorce.

Jerry lived with his mother and visited his father on weekends until he was fifteen. Everything was fine in Jerry's life until he became what he describes as "lazy around the house." He refused to do most of the chores his mother asked him to do because "I had my own things I wanted to do. I wanted to hang out with my friends and go places, and she didn't want me to do that because she needed help at home and she was working"; consequently, his equality masculine project momentarily began to decline. Indeed, during Jerry's seventh- and eighth-grade years his mother was not home when he returned from school because of her work. Jerry was supposed to use this time for homework and chores. He would usually do his homework but only a few chores, and then he would play with his friends. Jerry liked his friends because "they accepted me for who I was."

Q. What did you like to do with your friends?

A. Ride snowmobiles and practice shooting guns. We had fun together 'cause we never teased or fought.

Q. But you didn't do your chores?

A. Right. I'd slack off. I wouldn't do the dishes, walk the dog. I'd just watch TV or hang out with my friends, because I didn't want to do my chores. I was irresponsible.

Q. And your mother would continue to ask you to help out with the household duties?

A. Yeah. She'd say, "It's important that you learn to do this now, because when you're older there isn't going to be anybody that wants to take care of you." And I was like, "Whatever. I'll find somebody." And then she just kept nagging me and getting mad at me because I was lazy. So I finally told her "I want to move in with Dad."

Jerry moved in with his dad during the early part of his freshman year in high school. The bullying persisted in high school but Jerry reflexively chose to never respond in a violent way. The "walking away" reaction continued to work and he felt comfortable using it. The most frequent verbal bullying Jerry experienced in high school was being "called a fag a lot, and queer, and anything pertaining to being homosexual. So I just shrug it off. I could yell at the kid or something, but there's no point. He is just going to be narrow-minded about it. So I just turn my back on it instead of putting up the dukes." Accordingly, in high school Jerry continued to be constructed as embodying a subordinate masculinity by the dominant bullies yet he responded by personally orchestrating an equality masculine response.

Jerry was bullied mostly by the dominant "popular guys"— as he puts it, "the tough guys, the athletes, the macho guys." When I asked Jerry if he wanted to be like the "popular guys" he said, "At first I did. But then Mom and Dad told me, 'Just be your own person.' And that had a lot of influence on me. Plus I never really liked sports."

Q. You never liked sports?

A. Not really organized sports. I liked playing hockey, but not for a team.

Q. You just didn't want to participate in the organized aspect of sports?

A. You know in high school I see the locker room camaraderie. They walk around and snap each other's asses with towels and everything. I'm not really interested in that. And there is a lot of macho crap that goes on in the locker room and everything, and I just don't want to be part of that.

Q. Tell me about the other cliques in your high school.

A. The jocks are the popular guys because they get in the news for accomplishments they make in sports. It's like, "Hey, did you see so and so in the news the other day?" And then there are the brains which most people ignore. And then there are the loaders.

Q. What are loaders?

A. They are the mostly druggies. They're into pot and stuff. And then there are the homies or G-funks, because G is for gangsta. The G-funks think they're the tough guys.

Q. Which group are you in?

A. I'm not in a group. I have some friends that are loaders; we are kinda the laid-back crowd. But I'm not in any group 'cause it's like they all have something to prove. I've got nothing to prove. I am who I am, and if they don't like it—too bad.

Jerry also stated that there are numerous "feminine boys" in his school and, not surprisingly, "some" homophobia as well. Most people ignore these boys but occasionally they call them "fags."

Q. Are these boys gay?

A. I don't know if they are gay but they are kinda feminine. I get along with them real well but some guys constantly call them names like "fag" and "queer." I accept that some people are just like that.

Q. But you consider yourself heterosexual?

A. Yeah. I just never had a sexual interest in guys. When I was younger I liked to play with my friends but I like never saw it in a sexual way. It wasn't until around seventh grade that I started to like girls. I became interested in their body then.

In high school Jerry was yet to have a date (he described himself as a "virgin") but had numerous girl *friends*. "There are a bunch of girls at school that I get along with. I treat them just like anybody else, just like my friends. We talk about what's going on in life."

Q. Do you ever hear kids at school talking about engaging in sex?

A. Oh, yeah. I hear that a lot. But it's like, That's real tacky. If somebody is going to brag about that then I'm sorry to hear it. There is more to life than getting a piece of ass.

Q. So sexuality isn't something that is important to you?

A. I think sex is pretty much important to everybody. It's part of life, but not right now. I'm more interested in bringing my grades up in school than having sex.

Q. What are your plans after high school?

A. I'm going to have a family. I'm going to enjoy raising my kids. There are just so many things out there that I want to do that seem like fun. I'd love to race motorcycles. I'd love to have a dogsled team. There are just so many things out there that I'd love to do. I'm gonna start a business like Dad's, and then who knows where I could go!

Thus, Jerry continued to be labeled subordinate by the dominant boys because of his particular masculine construction in school. However, his interaction with the laid-back group and his other friends proved to reflect acceptance of his sex appearance and gender practices and, thus, in that peer group "site" Jerry's equality masculinity was thoroughly welcomed and embraced.

Karen

Karen is a tall, slim eighteen-year-old who has long blonde hair with highlights. To both interviews, she wore a small amount of makeup, tight jeans, slip-on shoes, and a colorful shirt. Karen is an extraordinarily articulate and self-confident girl who expressed much happiness—she smiled and laughed throughout both interviews. In what follows, I describe, through Karen's words, her family relations at home and her nonviolence at home, school, and in her peer group.

Family Relations

Karen grew up in what she refers to as "the perfect family," involving both biological parents and a brother, younger by three years. She lives in a large three-bedroom house in a working-class community and both parents work outside the home: "My dad is a mailman and my mom works at a bank." Karen expressed much closeness, love, and acceptance by both her parents and her brother. As she put it: "They would do anything for me." Moreover, the family always does things together:

In the summer we always go camping when my parents have vacation. We always go to the same camping spot by a lake. We love it there and we just go hiking, swimming, and just hang out. And during the winter we always go skiing—we're a real athletic family.

Karen and her brother have particular household chores which are gender specific. For example, Karen helps her mother cook and clean up in the kitchen, and her brother helps their father around the house, "fixing stuff, shoveling snow, cutting the grass, taking the garbage out, stuff like that." From Karen's point of view, then, there is a clearly established gender division of labor in her household, and as she continued: "My mom and I do all the girl stuff, like cooking, doing laundry, doing dishes, vacuuming, dusting, that kind of stuff, and my dad and brother do guy stuff, like heavy-lifting stuff, fixing stuff, and watching sports on TV." I asked Karen if she saw this as a problem and she replied, "Not at all. It's like we all have our stuff to do and we do it. No problems at all. It always works out." Thus, it is in this setting where Karen initially took up a fundamental feminine project as her own.

Nevertheless, Karen did indicate that although everyone has their individualized gendered chores, "Dad had the power in the house. My mom always gave in to him." I then asked Karen to expand on this point and she stated: "Mom and Dad always discuss stuff but in the end she always agrees with what Dad wants. It is like he's always right."

Q. Do they argue or discuss?

A. Never really any arguments or shouting, just talking and Dad winning out.

Q. How do you feel about that?

A. No problem, you know, they discuss stuff and it's just that Dad always is right, that's it.

Thus Karen's father embodied a localized hegemonic masculinity at home and her mother emphasized femininity. Karen also indicated that because she primarily interacts with her mother, "Mom is my number-one parent and also she has the most influence on me." I asked Karen to expand on this:

> Because we just really like doing stuff together. I like doing stuff with Dad but mostly I like doing stuff with Mom—you know, that girl thing.
>
> Q. What do you two do together?
>
> A. Doing stuff around the house, going shopping for food and clothes, you know, stuff like that.
>
> Q. And you enjoy that?
>
> A. Oh yeah. I really like being around Mom. I look up to her; she is really pretty, nice, smart, and kinda like my best friend, rather than a mom.
>
> Q. You then feel very close to her, right?
>
> A. For sure, I can talk with Mom about anything 'cause she's really nice and always listens and always has good advice.

Thus, Karen constructed a subordinate femininity in relation to her mother's dominating femininity at home.

Karen and I discussed any possible conflicts at home between her and her parents and her and her brother and she mentioned that "the major conflict is only between me and my brother—he likes to tease me and stuff. Just kinda sister and brother rivalry, nothing really major." Karen went on to point out that when this teasing occurs and "I get mad at him they [her parents] call a 'chill-out' session." Karen described a "chill-out session" as "we both have to go to our rooms, think about what we did, chill-out a little, and then come out and talk nicely with Mom and Dad about it." Karen said that both she and her brother would usually have to chill-out because her brother teased her and because she got mad at him. I then asked Karen if she also has conflicts with her parents, and this led to the following dialogue:

> Never. The only time I've had to chill-out is getting mad and shouting at my brother. Never with problems with Mom and Dad. My brother has.

Q. Can you give me an example?

A. Yeah, he argues with them a lot 'cause he always wants it his way. You know, he wants to hang out with his friends like until late at night and they won't let him, so he argues. And they just say, "Time for a 'chill-out' until you're ready to discuss in a nice way."

Q. Have you or your brother ever been spanked?

A. Never. Nobody in my family ever hits that I know about.

In short, Karen constructed at home a subordinate, accountably nonviolent femininity through congruence between her sex appearance and gender practices.

School, Peer Group, and Nonviolence

In elementary and middle school Karen had numerous friends—both boys and girls—who she reports having much fun with at school as well as after school. Karen did not play sports but rather, as she puts it: "I just did girl kinda stuff with my girlfriends, like play with dolls, dress up in high heels, short skirts, put lots a makeup on. My girlfriends and I would do that a lot and we loved it!" Karen also described getting along very well with teachers and doing quite well in school: "I've always been kind of a B+ student, never really got many A's at all."

Nevertheless, during the middle of her seventh-grade year Karen had gained considerable weight and she attributes this to the fact that she loves to cook and eat and "Mom and I did that all the time together. Lotsa goodies, so I got really fat!" Simultaneously, Karen noticed her girlfriends began to ignore her and not want to "hang out" with her. As she stated:

It was like I had girlfriends and then I didn't, you know. All of a sudden we weren't friends anymore. And one girl just said to me, "I don't like you anymore."

Q. Did your girlfriends explain why?

A. No, they'd just say mean things to me and whisper about me.

Q. What kind of things did they say?

A. They'd make mean comments about my weight. They'd call me "elephant" and sing that elephant song when I walk down the hall.

Q. What elephant song is that?

A. You know, it goes like [Singing to the tune of "Here We Go Round the Mulberry Bush"]: "The elephant goes like this and that, this and that, this and that, 'cause she's so big and she's so fat." They'd sing that, you know.

Q. Did they call you other names or act out in other ways?

A. Not really, just every day they'd call me elephant and in the hall they'd laugh at me, you know, look funny at me, whisper to each other, sing the song, and then just all laugh together. And then they just like totally rejected me and made rumors about me.

Q. Can you give me an example?

A. Yeah, like one girl was real nasty, like she would say that I got fat 'cause I was sleeping around so much with guys that I never got out of bed! That all I did is lay in bed and have sex with guys. And then some started calling me a "slut" and a "whore," when there is no way, you know, I was a virgin then!

Q. Did they bully you in any other way?

A. Yeah, they were all into sports and I wasn't at that time so they'd make nasty comments about that.

Q. Such as?

A. Oh, you know, stuff like, "You're too busy having sex to get in shape," and "A elephant can't play sports," stuff like that.

Q. How did you respond?

A. I just couldn't believe it 'cause it all seemed like a dream, you know. I didn't understand, like why do they all hate me now and say nasty stuff about me? I would go into the girls' bathroom and just cry. They were all like slim, pretty, into sports, and had lots a boyfriends. And I was just fat, no friends, didn't play sports, you know. So I just cried. And when I came out I would just like try to not see them, you know, try to avoid them as much as I could. I kinda became a loner, you know.

Despite her reflexive attempt to avoid the verbal and social bullies, Karen always seemed to be confronted by these girls in some way, every day, at school. The bullying continued throughout seventh and eighth grades and Karen reflexively experienced increasing sadness and loneliness, and because of the unrelenting verbal bullying, she even reflexively considered suicide several times during her eighth-grade year. It was during this time that Karen had more intense internal deliberations about how sad, depressed, and lonely she was, so eventually she reflexively decided to tell her mother everything in detail about the bullying and:

> Mom was real nice and understanding and she told me to just ignore them, you know, to just keep walking like they're not there. And the next day she went right to the school principal and he said he'd put a stop to it, but of course he never did. The nasty comments about me not playing sports, being the "school elephant" and a "slut," just kept going, every day. And my friends just kept rejecting me. But I tried to just ignore it, you know, not even look at them and just walk straight to class.

A few days following her meeting with the principal, Karen's mother asked her how things were now at school and Karen responded to that question by immediately crying while trying to put into words that "I can't take this anymore. I try to ignore it but I can't. It really hurts." However, Karen's mother immediately suggested "Plan B":

> She just real calmly told me that she had also gained weight and how about if we start to work out together at night. And I just started to laugh and cry at the same time 'cause I thought what a great idea and it made me so happy 'cause my mom was so caring. And so Mom got one of those exercise tapes and we'd exercise every night together before dinner and we also went on a diet.

Q. How did your dad and brother respond?

A. Actually my dad started cooking for him and my brother 'cause they didn't like what we ate. It was great, girl food and guy food for dinner!

Q. Did your mother suggest that you respond in some way to the bullies?

A. No, not at all. She never mentioned that. And I'm glad she didn't 'cause I wouldn't want to shout at them or call them names, or anything like that. That would just make things worse, you know.

Following the completion of her eighth-grade year, Karen and her mother continued their diet and exercise program so that by the end of the summer Karen had lost twenty pounds and was now back to her "normal" weight. She was extremely proud of this accomplishment and when she started high school she had to purchase a new wardrobe of school clothes "because all my old clothes were too big!" Thus, from Karen's point of view: "I wasn't fat anymore. It was great!"

Throughout middle school Karen was involved in swimming lessons and one of her instructors actually mentioned to her during the summer that she should try out for the high school swim team because she had "a perfect breaststroke and she said I was a 'natural.'" Subsequently Karen reflexively decided to talk with her mother and father about this and they thought it was a wonderful suggestion. My conversation with Karen about this development included the following:

Q. Did you try out for the team?

A. Yeah, right away. I love to swim; my brother and I did it all summer long and I got pretty good at it from my lessons.

Q. Did you make the team?

A. Yeah, and the coach thought I would be good at the breast-stroke events and the medley relay, you know, swim breast-stroke on the relay team. So I started to work out really hard and it was fun!

Q. How did your teammates treat you?

A. At first I was a little scared of what might happen 'cause there were some girls from my middle school on the team. A couple of times they would say stuff like, "watch out for waves 'cause the elephant is gonna dive in," but the other kids just looked confused when that happened 'cause I wasn't fat anymore and so they didn't know what it meant. And then one of my new friends said to the girl, "Why don't you swim against her if you're so cool?"

Q. And did the coach allow that?

A. Oh yeah, he actually liked when we did that, he'd call it a "challenge," and he said we should always be ready for a challenge at anytime just as a way to improve, you know. So the two of us and a couple of other freshman girls raced a hundred-meters breaststroke and I won!

Q. What did your teammates say?

A. They were like cheering me on and they all came up to me and gave me hugs and high fives and stuff after the race.

Q. Did the bully continue to bully you after that?

A. No, not at all. She came in last and a bunch of girls laughed at her so she never came back to the team.

Following this event, Karen was never the victim of bullying again and, in fact, "Now I had lots a friends again!" The dominant girls in Karen's high school consisted principally of girls involved in sports (including those on the swim team), and thus Karen became a practicing member of this dominant group. And toward the end of her first year in high school, Karen also began to date boys, especially boys on the swim team. Karen said she had first thought about boys and sexuality in middle school "but it didn't last long because all I could think about was avoiding people, you know, plus I had no friends, so I never really thought much about dating, plus boys didn't like me anyway, and if I did date them then my old friends even more would call me a 'slut.'" Karen attributed the change to her new swim team friends and their frequent "sex talk" about boys, "and what they thought about boys, who is nice, who is cute, who they didn't like, what they did on dates and hookups, stuff like that." Thus it was at this time that Karen explicitly began to attach a hetero-sexual project to her femininity and she reflexively decided to join in the above girls' group "sex talk." Karen expands on this topic below, noting how she is now "doing" dominant hetero-femininity:

> After I lost weight, joined the team, and got in shape I had lots a girlfriends and boyfriends. It was like every weekend I would be going out with different guys and then I really liked this one guy and I lost my virginity with him.
>
> Q. How did that happen?
>
> A. Just in his car going at it and we just did it, you know. I really felt close to him and liked him a lot. He was real nice and cute and he cared for me. He was the top boy swimmer and he'd help me with my stroke, so we really hit it off.
>
> Q. Did you talk to anyone about this boy?
>
> A. Yeah, of course. I told Mom all about him and what we did and she was like really understanding and just said that's how Dad and her did it the first time! We talked about birth control and stuff and she helped me get set up with that.
>
> Q. Did you talk with anyone else?
>
> A. Yeah, for sure, with my best friends. I didn't go into detail, just told them we did it and it was nice, it felt good. And they told me about what they did with their boyfriends, you know. And we also talked about birth control and stuff.

Karen indicated that now she had a large group of close friends—both boys and girls—who would "hang out together at school, you know in the hall, in the cafeteria, and in the library." Moreover, every weekend there would be a party at someone's house, "and we'd listen to music, dance, and just party and have fun." These friends were also the dominant boys and girls in her school and I asked Karen if any of these boys and girls ever bullied her and she replied, "No way. No more of that. We are all in good shape and stuff and good swimmers, good athletes, you know, so we just say nice things to each other, like 'You really look good tonight' or 'You're really hot tonight,' you know, stuff like that. We all look good and we all like each other and get along great. I have a great time in high school!" In short, Karen now constructed an accountably nonviolent dominant hetero-femininity at school.

Gender Conformity and Nonviolence at Home

What do these two life stories teach us about the relationship among sex, gender, sexuality, and nonviolence in the home setting? Regarding Jerry, we "see" him confronting the constraints and possibilities established through structured egalitarian gender relations at home, and his adoption of certain forms of social action. Jerry's embodied practices at home articulated with both his mother and father—they "did everything together"—engaging in such practices as hunting and fishing, cooking meals, and gardening. Thus, the salient available practices in the home milieu that Jerry engaged in consisted of both "masculine" and "feminine" chores and leisure activities. Jerry constructed an equality masculinity at home that aligned with his male appearance—because it is an accountable form of masculinity in this setting—and such embodied masculinity helped reproduce in-home egalitarian gender relations; Jerry was an accountable gender conformist in this setting. Moreover, Jerry had frequent conversations with his parents about sexuality and thus he seemingly constructed an egalitarian heteromasculinity project in this setting as he confidently, and for the most part unreflexively, embodied an equality masculine presence and *place* at home that was calm, routine, nonviolent, and sometimes "lazy."

Karen confronted the constraints and possibilities established through structured patriarchal gender relations at home (father ultimately had the power) alongside a comparable gender division of labor—Karen and her mother do "girl stuff" and her father and brother do "guy stuff." Thus, the "girl stuff" represents the salient available practices in the home milieu that Karen engaged in. Not surprisingly, at home Karen interacts primarily with her mother, who Karen described as her "best friend." Given that Karen successfully engaged in the available feminine practices at home, her embodied femininity never was challenged in this milieu by mother, father, or brother. Karen was accountably feminine at home and engaged in situationally subordinate feminine conduct that aligned with her female appearance—Karen was subordinate in relation to her mother's dominant femininity and her father's hegemonic masculinity—and such embodied femininity helped reproduce in-home gender relations; Karen was an accountable gender conformist in this setting. Distancing herself from the masculine practices of her father and brother, Karen confidently, and for the most part unreflexively, embodied a nonviolent feminine presence and *place* at home.

Repression, Reflexivity, and Recognition

Like the interviewees in chapters 3 and 4, both Jerry and Karen grew up in homes whereby they were considered "gender conformists" and neither personally experienced assaultive or sexual violence at home nor did they engage in any form of violence in this setting. However, within the setting of the school, and also like the previous four interviewees, a social process developed involving repression, reflexivity, and recognition, yet despite being labeled "gender and sexual deviants," the result was different from the interviewees in chapters 3 and 4 as both engaged in nonviolence. Let me briefly outline this social process and thus pathway to nonviolence.

Repression

As with the youth discussed in chapters 3 and 4, both Jerry and Karen experienced peer interaction in the social setting of the school that oppressively accentuated a very specific type of verbal and social bullying that centered on the body and featured a perceived imbalance between sex category and gender behavior. What these interview data show is that the meaning assigned by the in-school dominant bullies to Jerry's and Karen's *gender behavior* is influenced through their *perceived sex category*. In other words, for both Jerry and Karen, because their sex category was judged to be incongruent with their gender behavior, they subsequently became victims of gender and sexual repression through consistent bullying.

For Jerry, there was an imbalance between his perceived male category and his alleged unmanly behavior and body (e.g., initially he did not "fight back"; he did not play sports; and he had a "chubby" body). In other words, Jerry's body size and shape and his bodily behavior were viewed by the bullies as controverting his perceived sex category. According to the bullies, Jerry simply was a "fat ass," a "wimp," a "fag," and a "queer," who therefore "failed" to accomplish dominant masculinity in terms of appropriate bodily display and practice. Yet, because he was identified as a "male," he was consistently repressed through bullying victimization. And with Jerry we clearly notice the intersection of gender and sexuality: the subordinated sexual terms of "fag" and "queer" are attributed to him for not displaying and practicing "proper" dominant heteromasculinity.

For Karen, there was an imbalance between her perceived female category and her alleged unwomanly body—according to the bullies, she had a "fat" body, she was labeled "elephant," "slut," and "whore," and she did not play sports. Consequently, Karen's body size and shape were viewed by the bullies as controverting her perceived sex category—Karen "failed" to accomplish femininity in terms of bodily display and practice, yet because she was identified as "female," she was consistently repressed through bullying victimization. And like Jerry, Karen's victimization represents the intersection of gender and sexuality: the subordinated sexual terms of "slut" and "whore" are attributed to her for not initially practicing "proper" dominant heterofemininity.

For both Jerry and Karen, then, their *body* and their *bodily behavior* conveyed a sex/gender combined image at school that the bullies viewed as an imbalance between sex category and gender/sexual display and behavior. At home, both were practicing gender conformists, yet at school, they were now labeled gender and sexual deviants. And it was this situationally recognized bodily imbalance by the dominant bullies at school and their attempt at repression—as conveyed through their verbal and social bullying—that *motivated* Jerry and Karen to engage in reflexivity, to which we now turn.

Reflexivity

Initially, Jerry reflexively felt subordinate, small, and insecure from the consistent bullying, and thus he decided to become a loner rather than seek out companionship and friendships. Eventually the distress from the bullying became unbearable which led Jerry, through internal conversations, to decide to "handle playground business" in the situationally "appropriate" masculine way; that is, to physically "fight back." Jerry determined that he wanted to exhibit a "tough" masculine persona, and he decided that his tall body could *facilitate* such masculine agency. So Jerry reflexively engaged in numerous playground fights and, although he "won some and lost some," the bullying by dominant boys continued unabated. Karen reflexively realized initially that her body *restrained* her agency: she could not live up to the in-school dominant heterofeminine expectations of a slim body, having boyfriends, and participating in sports. This was internally distressing to her, and initially she did not know how to solve the problem. So Karen reflexively decided to become a loner at school.

Jerry's and Karen's bodies then were actually participating in their reflexive agency by suggesting possible courses of social action: Jerry initially decided to "fight back" against the bullies, and Karen physically avoided the bullies by becoming a loner. Frustrated, and given the continuing distressing situation, both reflexively decided to turn to their parents for help. And both learned when and how to use their bodies in a new and gendered way. For both Jerry and Karen, then, their bodies became objects of their reflexive social action: Jerry, given specific directions how to use his body, in particular he was advised to "walk away"; Karen was advised to ignore the bullies and simply "walk past" them without acknowledging their presence. And

Karen's body became the object of her reflexive social action as she attempted to transform it into a feminine body "appropriate" to her specific school setting by engaging in an exercise-and-dieting program.

During this intensified reflexivity, then, both Jerry and Karen came to internally conceptualize themselves in the way that others perceived them—they reified the images communicated by others. Much of this reflexive conceptualization was arrived at by way of interaction and communication with others. Through such interaction and communication, both Jerry and Karen took an "external" view of themselves, thus becoming the objects of their own reflexivity. Because of the shame and mortification they suffered from bullying victimization, an assault upon their self-definition and social identification emerged. This assault drove them to move from an unconcerned and indifferent relationship with their bodies to a more enhanced, reflexive one. In other words, they internalized the "external" by engaging in reflexivity; in the process, they both determined their course of action in relation to their bodies and to their social circumstances.

In short, Jerry and Karen reflexively deliberated about their individual social circumstances at school—which was significantly different from their interactions at home—and, in particular, reflected on their bodies to determine what they could and could not "do" in the school setting to overcome their subordinating social situations. Accordingly, their bodies became reflexive participants in the generating and shaping of their social practices.

Recognition

Extending his reflexivity into social action, Jerry responded to the bullying by internally deciding to "do experiments" whereby he simply would "walk away." Like the other boys in this study, shame and inadequacy threatened Jerry's masculine self as revealed in his reflexivity. Electing to "walk away" rather than "fight back" was an attempt at validation by embodying a specific masculine self for his audience and for himself—it was an attempt to reduce/offset the subordinating interactions and feelings produced at school, yet simultaneously it constructed a new nonviolent equality form of masculinity. By reflexively deciding to "walk away" rather than physically challenge the bullies, Jerry orchestrated the embodiment of a powerfully peaceful impartial masculinity in the eyes of others. He reflexively hoped this new bodily practice would facilitate a tenacious yet composed masculine agency and eradicate the "wimp" label. Nevertheless, because of a socially identified imbalance between sex category and gender behavior, Jerry was subjected continually to derogatory verbal bullying. In fact, in high school he was now labeled "fag" and "queer." However, such bullying no longer reinforced feelings of masculine inadequacy because for him "walking away" proved to secure a stronger masculine response than that presented by the bullies. Indeed, his body now *facilitated* a new nonviolent equality (and celibate) masculine agency in the in-school social setting, which Jerry determined was a valid and unique form of masculine *recognition*—and it was supported and fully recognized by his subordinate "laid-back" friends; he was a gender conformist in this setting—yet the dominant bullies did not concur with his embodied equality masculinity as they continually constructed Jerry as a "gender deviant." Thus, within the "site" of the school, two different youth groups "read" Jerry in two different ways, one celebrating and the other repressing his gender practice. Nevertheless, because of his accountability in the laid-back group, Jerry reflexively felt comfortable with his nonviolent and celibate equality masculinity—from his and his friends' point of view, his sex appearance and gender practices were congruent—and, therefore, Jerry reflexively devoted himself to, and practiced regularly, this masculinity, even when bullied. Indeed, neither masculine violence nor heterosexual performance was *salient* to his sense of self within the setting of his laid-back peer group.

Karen extended her reflexivity by deciding to diet and exercise and eventually to use her swimming talents to join the high school swim team. Karen's developed bodily skills at swimming allowed her to respond to oppressive verbal bullying by attempting to make use of a "swim challenge." Reflexively deciding to participate in the challenge that a friend organized,

Karen ended up winning the swim race. She was accepted by the other girls and boys on the team, developed close friendships among these girls and boys, became a practicing member of the dominant heterofeminine girls' clique, and the verbal bullying disappeared completely.

Karen's body now *facilitated* dominant heterofeminine agency, an agency that constructed a more confident sense of self, a new way of interacting with and through her body in the school setting. Karen constructed a new heterofeminine self through her embodied practices at school, and she was successful. Karen's actual accomplishment of dominant heterofemininity (e.g., she was an excellent swimmer, she was popular, and she attracted much sexual attention from boys) meant that there no longer existed in the opinion of co-present interactants an imbalance between her sex appearance and gender behavior; Karen was now an accepted, practicing member of the dominant popular girls' clique at school. Like Kelly (chapter 3), Karen now possessed a different body and a new heterofeminine self. Karen practiced specific bodily skills (e.g., swimming and dating) and thus she literally created an accountable way of personifying heterofemininity in and through her body. And because Karen's perceived sex category continued to influence the meaning assigned to her bodily display and behavior, she was now conceptualized at school as a gender conformist. Because she now had many friends—both girls and boys—Karen gained wholehearted *recognition* as heterofeminine in the in-school social setting. Differing from Jerry, in Karen's dominant girls' group, heterosexuality remained a *salient* social practice, yet Karen accomplished heterofemininity, in part through her consistent dating and participation in "sex talk" at school.

In chapter 6, I will discuss Jerry and Karen more thoroughly, especially in relation to the other four life histories presented in this book.

6

Conclusion

As I discussed in chapter 1, the emergence of a two-sex model gave rise to a cultural emphasis on male genitalia as now different from female genitalia in *kind* rather than in *degree*, and this new difference signified an essential bodily distinction between men and women. In other words, the "truth" of *two and only two sexes*—as well as the accompanying naturally opposite and complementary heterogenders—is fashioned primarily through the application of genitalia as the ultimate criterion in making sex assignments. Our recognition of another's *sex* then is dependent upon the presentation of visible bodily characteristics—a combined bodily sex and gender presentation that becomes the substitute for the concealed genitalia. Consequently, although biological differences clearly exist between male and female bodies, during social interaction sex is always already a social interpretation. That is, sex is achieved through the application and social acceptance of identifying characteristics that proclaim one as "male" or "female." The meaning of sex then is socially "read" through interpretations placed on the visible body; during social interaction there exists a prior belief in *two and only two sexes*, which then motivates a search for its support. As Suzanne Kessler and Wendy McKenna (1978: 7) put it, "The element of social construction is primary in all aspects of being female and male." Recognition of both "sex" and "gender" is always already a social act—part of everyday interaction—that occurs simultaneously. And consequently, during most interpersonal interactions, "sex" and "gender" are indistinguishable from one another because we unreflexively recognize their congruence.

However, people who present ambiguous "bodily emblems" of "sex"—such as transsexuals in transition from one sex to another—produce hesitation in an otherwise smooth social process of sex assignment and attribution. Yet by so doing, they simultaneously bring the social construction of sex (and gender) to light. The research reported in chapters 3, 4, and 5 adds further light to this social process because none of the six interviewees claimed transgender status nor did their peers have a problem recognizing their bodily presentation as male or female. Instead, according to co-present interactants within particular social settings (primarily at school), all six adolescents "failed" somehow to engage in gender and/or sexual behavior "appropriate" to their assigned sex. The six life stories then represent an interesting comparison for understanding the relationship among sex, gender, and sexuality because for these youth, in specific spaces, their *sex appearance* was judged to be incongruent with their *gender and/or sexual behavior*. Indeed, during social interaction we generally *read* sex/gender/(hetero)sexuality as an inextricable, seamless whole, and this is why incongruence produces a cognitive dissonance in us for which people like the six adolescents discussed herein get punished.

In addition to the above, by examining the different "sites" of home, school, street, peer group, and park, we can capture the fluidity of the relationship between sex appearance and gender/sexual behavior and the changing nature of acceptance and rejection of particular social practices. And such a comparative analysis of the six life stories has richly revealed that (1) social interaction and interpretation in specific sites shape the character, definition, and meaning of sex/gender/sexuality; (2) social interaction relies on the inseparability of sex appearance and gender/sexual behavior; (3) given the nature of the interaction, an imbalance in sex appearance and gender/sexual behavior *may* motivate assaultive or sexual violence; and (4) the significance of gender and sexuality shift from context to context; that is, gender and sexuality are not absolutes and are not always equally salient in every social setting in which individuals participate.

Accordingly, to be "read" by others as heteromasculine/ feminine, each adolescent in this study was required to ensure that their proffered selves presented a balance between sex appearance and gender/sexual behavior. The meaningfulness of accomplishing heteromasculinity/femininity was based on the reaction of others to their sex *and* gender/sexual embodiment, and whether or not this embodiment was judged accountable was highly important to their sense of self. Embodied accountability is vital to any individual's situational recognition as a competent social agent. If an individual's sex appearance and gender/sexual behavior are categorized publicly by others as inconsonant (such as through bullying), that degradation may result in a spoiled heterogender self-concept (Goffman 1968). It was this situationally recognized "failure" by contextually powerful individuals that reflexively motivated all six adolescents, in different ways, to engage in assaultive/sexual violence or nonviolence to *correct* the subordinating social situation. Given that such interaction questioned, undermined, and threatened individual heteromasculinity/ femininity, each youth reflexively assumed that only contextually "appropriate" (hetero)masculine/feminine practices were *the* means of overcoming the bullying challenge.

In chapter 1 I also posed the question: How are gender and sexuality *related* to sex? The data reported here suggest the following answer: practicing heteromasculinity/femininity relies on the coexistence of *sex* appearance and *gender/sexual* behavior. When sex appearance and gender/sexual behavior are congruent—or accepted by those in power to be harmonious—heteromasculinity and heterofemininity are validated and heterogender conformity occurs. However, when sex appearance does not align with gender/sexual behavior—and that nonalignment is emphasized by those in power—heteromasculinity/femininity may be questioned and gender/sexual deviance results. And, in addition, *reactive* violence is more likely to occur when there is a consistent publicly pronounced imbalance between sex appearance and gender/sexual behavior.

The evidence from this study, then, suggests that feminist criminologists and sociologists should focus on "embodied gender/ sexuality," or the confluence and symbiosis of sex appearance and gender/sexual behavior in the social validation or invalidation of heteromasculinity and heterofemininity—rather than concentrating solely on gender. *Embodied gender/sexuality* is an interactive process involving both a sex and gender/sexuality presentation and a reading of that presentation by co-present interactants. Particular forms of embodied gender/sexuality emerge in specific settings and, therefore, shift over time and across sites. In all of the various sites these adolescents participated in, the social perception of both sex and heterogender were salient to "seeing" heteromasculinity/ femininity. Consequently, one's embodied gender/sexuality is interactively and situationally produced simultaneously through sex appearance and gender/sexual behavior.

But in addition, all six of the life stories reveal that the body is an inescapable and integral part of practicing heteromasculinities/femininities. All of the adolescents' bodies participated in social action by delineating courses of social conduct. Their bodies were not neutral in their reflexive social action but rather were *agents* of social practice in that they constrained and eventually enabled particular forms of gendered/sexual social action; their bodies mediated and influenced internal conversations and thus future social practices. Given the context (at school, for instance), each of the six adolescents reflexively determined that their bodies would do certain things but not others. All six bodies were reflexively *lived* in terms of what they could "do." Yet their bodies were a necessary and mediate component of their social action (see further, Connell 1995).

The various violent and nonviolent social practices of the six interviewees were shaped by those around them in the different "sites," and it is the social embodied practices of co-present interactants that are their source of knowledge and information about the "appropriate" embodied behavior. And in seeking acceptance from co-present interactants, all six adolescents were involved in a "struggle for recognition" (Mead 1967), engaged as they were in embodied practices that were shaped by the practices and opinions of co-present interactants, hoping that these very same peers would recognize and accept their sex/gender/sexuality presentation. All six boys and girls entered into an intensified reflexivity by internalizing and deliberating about their embodied social experiences, initially in the "site" of the school. They mulled over the problem of bullying at school, its relation to their bodies, considered how this made them feel, planned and decided what to do, prioritized what mattered most, and assessed how others would respond (Archer 2007). Finally, they each reflexively chose certain contextually "appropriate" social actions to end the bullying, each seeking to eradicate their gender/sexual deviance and to gain *recognition*—either privately or publicly—as gender/sexual conformists.

The six personal stories also confirm how secondary schools (as well as other sites) maintain heteronormativity. For example, through interaction at school, a discourse was formed communicating that a male/female equals masculine/feminine equals heterosexual alignment is normal and natural and that alternative sex/gender/sexuality alignments are abnormal and unnatural. The consequence is that boys and girls are bound to face many types of bullying (verbal, physical, and social) exacted for "failure" to conform to situationally "appropriate" sex/gender/sexuality displays/behaviors. Accordingly, this bullying helps maintain unequal, structured heterogender relations within the school (as well as other sites). Boys and girls who do not display the "appropriate" embodied alignment through presentation and practices, and who do not use, or have no interest in using, their bodies in a particular way (such as sports), frequently experience distress and frustration due largely to verbal/social/physical bullying. These boys and girls represent subordinated forms of gender and sexuality, in that they are designated the inferior "Others" because their "sex" is defined as not aligning with their "gender/sexuality."

Arguably, then, gender and sexual hegemony constructs a hierarchy among boys, among girls, and between boys and girls, based on incongruity between sex/gender/sexuality. And this structure at school establishes and enforces the gender/sexual practices available for "proper" sex/gender/sexuality embodiment, and it's precisely this system that figured significantly in

the six narratives as the major site for gender/sexual confronta-
tion, reflexive embodied social action, structured gender/sexual
relations, and eventual violence/nonviolence.

In addition to the above, the interview data discussed in
chapters 3, 4, and 5 yield certain additional compelling findings.
In what follows I discuss six such salient conclusions and how
each suggests future directions in feminist criminological and
sociological research. I close the chapter by briefly suggesting
several crucial social policies for curbing bullying—and thus its
partner, reactive youth violence—in secondary schools.

Sexual and Assaultive Violence

In this section I revisit the cases of Sam and Lenny to compare
sexual and assaultive violence by two boys. Let me begin with
Sam and add some important features to our discussion and
thus understanding of his involvement in sexual violence. One
of the dominant themes reported in the feminist literature on
"normative heterosexuality" is the existence of an alleged *natural* "male sexual drive" discourse that has a widespread and
forceful cultural influence on the sexuality of boys and men
as well as girls and women (Hollway 1984; Gavey 2005). This
"male sexual drive" discourse is the culturally dominant and
normative way of understanding sexuality by boys and men in
Western societies, and it emphasizes that the asserted "need" or
"urge" to engage in sexuality is a "strong, almost overwhelming drive that exists in all healthy normal men" and therefore
"men will go to great lengths to have sex (including paying for
it)" (Gavey 2005: 104).

Regarding heterosexuality, implicit in this discursive notion
of a natural "male sexual drive" is the perception that boys and
men instinctively are the sexual initiators and aggressors while
the role of girls and women is to receive or resist such sexual
advances—girls and women are charged as the gatekeepers
who "set the limits" on heterosex (Gavey 105). As Nicola Gavey
(105) further states, girls'/women's agency within the context
of the "male sexual drive" discourse "is limited to the extent of

responding to (or perhaps anticipating) the man's needs and initiatives. That is, her actions are premised on the basis of meeting, or denying, his sexual pleasure, rather than acting to advance her own." Heterosexual boys and men adhering to this discursive "male sexual drive" then come to believe that legitimately they are "entitled" to apply pressure on girls and women—culturally this is viewed as "normal" seduction—to overcome any resistance from girls/women, and thus to eventually "score."[1]

The life-history data discussed in chapter 4 reveal that prior to, during, and immediately after the sexual violence by Sam, such a "male sexual drive" arguably was embedded in his reflexive perception that his crime was not sexual violence but, rather, a legitimate way to "do" heteromasculinity. From Sam's perspective, then, he constructed a specific type of permissible heteromasculinity: a dominating and controlling form that centered on sexual conquest of the girls he babysat. Sam was in "need" of "some kind of sexual experience" and he reflexively chose to babysit younger girls to accomplish this goal. Sam used manipulation strategies to gain sexual access to the girls he was babysitting—to triumph over their resistance—and he reflexively felt entitled to such sexual access. Recall Sam's comment: "I felt like I should be able to have sexual contact with anybody that I wanted to. And I couldn't do that with girls my own age. So I felt like, okay, I'll get it from girls I was babysitting." And Sam decided he was entitled to sex because: "I'm a guy. I'm supposed to have sex. I'm supposed to be like every other guy." Sam defined "having sex" as involving girls providing sexual pleasure to him through fondling and oral sex, and when he "successfully" manipulated the interaction so that this occurred, he saw himself as super-heteromasculine. Sam reflexively concluded that he was "better" than the "cool guys" because he had complete control over the girls he babysat. Sam internally visualized the "cool guys" involved in sexual relationships whereby their partner "can say what she wants and she has a choice. But the girls I babysat didn't have the choice. It was like I made it look like they had a choice, but when they stated their choice, if they said no, I like bugged them and bugged them until they didn't say no." Sam eroticized domination over "his" powerless "partners" because from Sam's point of view he was entitled to use as much manipulative coercion as possible to obtain sexual pleasure from the girls he babysat—Sam was moved to engage in this crime by his reflexive belief in the "male sexual drive" discourse. In Sam's life history then we are able to "see" how he *created* a situation in which he was in masculine control and in which he could not be rejected by "feminizing" boys and girls—no matter how his body appeared or acted; as Sam stated: "There was no way I could get rejected." Finally, Sam's comment, "I felt like a girl," is important because by presenting a clear and definite heterosexual identity through sexual violence—if only privately to him—any vestige of the feminine is squashed and Sam is able to claim not simply a credible, but a superlative, embodied masculine presence. In short, Sam constructed a nonthreatening context in which heteromasculinity could be performed according to the in-school dominant criteria. And Sam's life story suggests that future research on sexual violence by boys and men should closely examine how the "male sexual drive" discourse, as an aspect of normative heterosexuality, *may* be embedded in their reflexive deliberations and thus in their motivations and justifications for sexual violence.

Sam's life story also challenges perspectives that conceptualize sexual violence as simply the personification of male power. Sam unmistakably lacked masculine power—that is, vis-à-vis other boys at school—and the resulting sexual violence was motivated to realize embodied domination and power over his victims *and* to be heterosexual in a superior way to the "real guys." Unfortunately, criminological research has paid little attention, if any, to the social and criminal practices of subordinate boys who have been labeled "wimp" or "fag." Accordingly, Sam's life history suggests that future research should include work on sexual violence by heterosexual subordinate boys, that is, boys labeled "heterosexual wimps" who are constructed bodily as not heteromasculine but who nevertheless are sexually attracted to girls.

Lenny's eventual assaultive violence presents an interesting difference from Sam's story. Like Sam, Lenny was often bullied at school for his physical size and shape and for not demonstrating that he was "a man." Lenny accepted the in-school cultural notion that being masculine meant responding to provocation with physical violence. But because he was physically small and obese relative to the bullies, Lenny was unable to respond in such a "manly" fashion. However, this does not mean that Lenny simply accepted this powerless position. On the contrary, when taunted by physically smaller and weaker boys at school and in his neighborhood, Lenny reflexively turned to assault as a response. Through his internal deliberations, Lenny prudently decided to avert retaliating against the bullies while carefully creating a situation in which his masculine domination would be "successful." Thus Lenny reflexively chose the hallway at school and the street in his neighborhood as appropriate "sites" for physical domination of other boys because in these settings the violence, he hoped, would be confirmed by his peers. Although it did not work out completely as he wished—some in the "audience" at school told him to "pick on" someone his own size—Lenny was able to satisfy his father's criteria for doing appropriate masculine violence and he was "successful" on the street. Thus his fear of being seen as a "wimp" and his resulting low masculine self-esteem motivated Lenny to deny masculinity in "others." Consequently, Lenny's story suggests the importance of future research on why certain subordinate "heterosexual wimps" respond to bullying by turning specifically to assaultive violence outside the school context.

However, Lenny's story also begs an important question: Given his school definition as "wimp," why did Lenny, unlike Sam, not engage in sexual violence? The answer, I believe, is at least twofold. First, Lenny had access to boys who were smaller and weaker than himself—boys he could physically assault. Lenny's reflexive agency, in part, was recognizing such boys and selecting the appropriate site for his body to conduct itself in the appropriate physically masculine way. Indeed, in the hallway at school and on the street in his neighborhood, Lenny was applauded by his mentor (father) for demonstrating his physical capabilities. Sam differed from Lenny in that he was never able to demonstrate toughness through physical aggression against any other *boys*. Second, Lenny's conception of sexuality and therefore heteromasculinity differed from that of Sam. Again, the reason is twofold. First, sexuality is not important to Lenny; as he stated, one does not need to be sexual to be "cool." For Sam, sexuality was a crucial component of daily life and being heterosexually active was essential to his masculinity. Moreover, because Lenny's brother was gay and Lenny recognized him as 100 percent masculine, heterosexuality was not connected to masculinity as it was for Sam—*the "male sexual drive" was not a salient feature in Lenny's reflexivity and sense of self*. Thus, Lenny's life history challenges views arguing that normative heterosexuality and thus the "male sexual drive" requires "unremitting confirmation" by boys and men (Britton 2011: 39). Indeed, Lenny's life story suggests that future research should address the contextual *salience* of sexuality, examining in which social situations heterosexuality and the "male sexual drive" discourse become significant to social interaction and eventually sexual violence, and in which social settings they do not. Second, Lenny's father emphasized, and Lenny accepted, that masculinity is not related to violence against women—"It's okay to hit boys but not girls." Therefore bodily control of girls was conceptualized as outside the reflexive realm of Lenny's heteromasculine self and practices. Consequently, Lenny was defined socially as a "heterosexual wimp" who used *assaultive* violence—rather than *sexual* violence—in an attempt to nullify his subordinate masculine status at school. And Lenny's life story points to the necessity of future research on subordinate "heterosexual wimps" and why they engage in certain types of crime and violence.

Disrupting Difference

Kelly's life history is especially interesting because she constructed a fundamental masculine gender project by, in part, displaying herself in a masculine way, engaging primarily in what she and others in her milieu consider to be authentically masculine behavior, and outright rejecting most aspects of femininity. Notwithstanding, the case of Kelly raises interesting questions regarding girls' construction of masculine practices in certain settings and whether or not under relations of gender inequality girls actually can become accountably masculine. The inequalities Kelly experienced in the "badass group" ensured that Kelly's experience as a masculine badass-group member could never be the same as the boys' in that specific setting. This was particularly evident in the heterosexual meanings of the group, where Kelly experienced a dilemma about sexuality—she had to be asexual in that setting in order to sustain masculine accountability. Accordingly, Kelly's masculine self was different qualitatively from that of the badass boys as she did not "do" masculinity within the same bodily terms as the boys. Thus, Kelly's masculinity was *different* qualitatively (and could only be so) from the masculinity of the badass boys—Kelly constructed masculinity but *not* heteromasculinity. Thus, we "see" in Kelly's life story how the salience of heterosexuality prominently appears within the context of both school ("dyke") and the badass group yet is constructed differently in each setting.[2] Kelly's experiences then suggest that future research not simply investigate the situational salience of (hetero)sexuality, but where, when, and how that salience differs by both boys and girls.

In addition to the above, Kelly was constituted as a different kind of badass-group member because her body was subordinate in the sense of allegedly being unable to participate adequately in violence. For example, because Kelly did not "pass" as a "real" male, she was "allowed" to participate only in certain forms of group violence—those where the boys determined Kelly would not get in the way or be hurt (she was disallowed participation in *all* robberies and burglaries)—and this worked against her as a fully embodied and accountably masculine member of the group. In other words, Kelly was conceptualized as "unfeminine" but not "unfemale." Consequently, and although Kelly strove to "blend in" and to avoid bodily characteristics that might reinforce girl stereotyping—that is, she *attempted* to be accountably masculine—she still was seen by the boys as deficient in certain ways, primarily in terms of perceived "sex." Because gender power pervaded perceptions of individual performance in the badass group, the boys laid claim to what bodily characteristics were sufficiently accountable. Kelly behaved in broadly similar ways as the boys in the group (even participating in the power barfs!), attempting to replicate preexisting masculine practices. In addition, Kelly's bodily display was constructed to symbolize gender opposition to femininity. For example, Kelly wore boyish clothing, as demonstrated in her deemphasizing of her breasts, waist, and legs (through loose-fitting clothes) and shaving the back of her head. Although Kelly communicated opposition to femininity and the embrace of masculinity, she also actually attempted to nullify her femaleness—she never wanted to look or act like a girl. Kelly's body being the primary site on which to inscribe the negation of femaleness, she quite literally attempted to erase any notion of femininity by concealing socially defined female attributes (also see Ekins and King 2006). And a situationally constructed masculine bodily display was the *only* possibility with which to facilitate such an erasure.

Despite her fighting ability and de-emphasizing her gender difference, because she did not "pass" completely as male, the "real" male body remained the standard that positioned "unreal" female bodies as "out of place." In other words, Kelly's life story showed that which characteristics, practices, and bodies qualify as masculine is a political question. Accordingly, Kelly was subordinated and excluded from power in the group because she was not completely accountably masculine according to those with the power to make such a determination. Kelly's life story demonstrates how gender hegemony is established in localized settings, like a badass group, through the social construction of "sex," and thus "male" bodies are determined to be "superior" to "inferior" bodies, even when "female" bodies actively engage in the same practices as "male" bodies. This unique construction of localized hegemonic masculinity is a significant area requiring future research.

Consequently, although Kelly's embodied practices in the three milieus of home, school, and badass group did not completely *erase* gender difference, they did *disrupt* it. Kelly's story raises a seminal question: If girls and women do not completely "pass" as "male," can they ever escape difference? Kelly clearly did not, as she was disallowed entrance into the same masculine *place* in gender relations as the badass boys. Thus, it is important to underline that drawing attention solely to differences among girls/women, and/or similarities between boys/men and girls/women, can make it difficult to understand how women's *collective* disadvantage may be institutionalized in particular settings, such as a teenage badass group. Kelly provides evidence of the complicated and diverse nature of sex/gender embodiment and moves us beyond the masculine/feminine dichotomy toward the recognition of alternative gender dimensions. Indeed, this complexity and variety in Kelly's sex/gender appearance and practice disrupts the notion of only two oppositional gender categories, and challenges perspectives that conflate sex and gender.

Kelly's life story indicates that during early childhood she engaged mostly in what she called "boyish" behavior—eventually embodying an in-home subordinate yet accountable masculinity—and within the settings of school and the badass group she combined masculine and feminine appearance and practices. Although clearly embodying a masculine *presence*, yet also rejected by her peers at school, the boys and girls in the badass group recognized her uniqueness by referring to Kelly as "ladybug" (because male and female ladybugs look the same and perform the same activities) and fully accepted and integrated her into the group. Kelly of course did not enjoy complete gender and sexual equality—as noted, she had to remain asexual in the badass setting and her body was subordinated to the "male body"—yet through her agency she nevertheless carved out a special embodied gendered niche. Kelly steered an intermediate course in the badass-group context, interacting with and through her body as both masculine and feminine. Kelly appeared as a *gender blend*, cultivating an embodied androgynous self that constituted a different type of embodiment—*a social boy with a vagina*—and therefore a unique and intermediate *place* within the gender relations of the badass group. Kelly *disrupted* gender difference by approximating a boy but not fully becoming a boy; she embodied a gender neither masculine nor feminine, but situationally a novel combination. Not surprisingly, then, what the evidence on Kelly suggests is *gender diversity* rather than *gender dichotomy* and the need for further research to uncover not only more data on that gender variety but its relation to crime and violence as well.

Localized Hegemonic Masculinities

Kelly's life story also alerts us to the variety of ways localized hegemonic masculinities are contextually constructed. As indicated in the previous section, a particularized, localized hegemonic masculinity was orchestrated in Kelly's badass group. But in addition, in five of the interviewees' families (Jerry's family is the sole exception), all of the fathers/stepfathers embodied a localized hegemonic masculinity in relation to the mothers' emphasized femininity, and Kristen's life story indicates that she occasionally transformed into a "surrogate wife," practicing emphasized femininity in relation to her stepfather's hegemonic masculinity. In these three different examples, then, meanings of gender difference were materialized in the practices of boys/men and girls/women, publicly (yet locally) structuring and legitimating hierarchical superior/inferior gender relations between them. These differences in hegemonic masculinities at the local level suggest that future research would benefit by comparing various local "sites" to explicate the similarities and differences in hegemonic masculine constructions.

Notwithstanding, the relationship between the in-school dominant masculine bullies and Lenny, Sam, and Jerry, demonstrate how unequal masculine/feminine relations can likewise be established in and through exclusively "male" bodies. By means of verbal bullying, Lenny, Sam, and Jerry were momentarily invested with situationally defined "inferior" gender qualities that assimilated with femininity. This interaction then constructed fleeting hegemonic masculinities by legitimating and stabilizing a hierarchical and unequal gendered relationship between masculinity and femininity. Moreover, in addition to this obvious symbolic blurring with femininity, derogatory terms such as "fag" and "queer" simultaneously reproduce heteronormativity by negatively disparaging same-sex sexuality among boys.

Finally, Sam's sexual violence represents what we might label a *pseudo*-hegemonic masculinity, because the private character of his violence disallowed the public legitimation of the manifested unequal masculine/feminine interaction. To be sure, the gender effects of Sam's sexual violence inscribe the girls who embody weakness and vulnerability as feminine, and Sam, who embodies strength and invulnerability, as masculine, thus constructing inferior feminine victims and a superior masculine perpetrator. The result is a *pseudo*-hegemonic masculinity within the privacy of Sam's home.

What these different forms of localized—as opposed to regional and global—hegemonic masculinities suggest is the importance of examining all localized settings to examine the various and omnipresent nature of gender hegemony. Moreover, what the data in chapters 3, 4, and 5 further suggest is the importance of distinguishing masculinities that legitimate a hierarchical relationship between boys/men and girls/women, between masculinity and femininity, and among boys/men from those that do not. Hegemonic masculinities are unique among the diversity of masculinities, and making this distinction unambiguous will enable scholars to recognize and research the whole variety of nonhegemonic masculinities, such as the dominating masculinities identified between the fathers/stepfathers and Lenny and Sam, as well as the equality masculinities constructed by Jerry and his father.

Inequalities among Girls

Meda Chesney-Lind and Katherine Irwin (2008) recently reported their findings of interviews with twenty-seven young women, discovering that "'girlworld' can be a frightening and difficult terrain to traverse," girls often experiencing "being unwanted and unaccepted by their peers. Indeed, such threats are potent particularly because relationships tend to matter so much to girls" (33). Chesney-Lind and Irwin (39) conclude that "there are mean girls in the world, their primary targets are other girls, and the pain and disappointment inflicted have lingered even as young women enter adulthood." Surprisingly, however, although Chesney-Lind and Irwin (39–50) show that girls are often bullied—for example, because of their bodily shape and size (e.g., being "fully developed") and sexuality (e.g., labeled a "slut")—apparently these authors find such details insignificant inasmuch as they refrain from any reflection as to why. Similarly, notwithstanding reporting that the young women interviewed frequently disclosed being bullied by "popular" and "socially powerful" girls, Chesney-Lind and Irwin eschew any examination of the inequalities among girls and how such inequalities may be related to various forms of femininities, bullying, and thus crime and violence.

Kristen's life history, however, strikingly highlights the relationship between adolescent girl bullying, embodied heterofeminine inequalities, and eventual sexual offending. To be sure, the interview data exclusively point to the construction of dominant and subordinate femininities within the specific social settings in which Kristen participated. Kristen's personal story clearly confirms how adolescent social settings—such as those in which Kristen was involved—often maintain a "culture of cruelty" (Kindlon and Thompson 1999) whereby girls (and boys) face many types of bullying (verbal, physical, and social) exacted for failure to conform to certain sex/gender/sexuality displays/behaviors, and that this bullying helps maintain and sustain unequal structured relations among girls, among boys, and between boys and girls, within these settings. For girls specifically, considerable research shows that the tall, slim, and sporty girls in junior high and high school usually are the most popular—admired by peers (and parents and teachers) for their bodies and athletic abilities—and set the standards for dominant feminine display and behavior (Bettis and Adams 2005). Dominant femininity constructed by adolescent girls no longer centers on such embodied practices as submissiveness, docility, and passivity. Instead, today such characteristics as self-control, determination, competition, and athleticism, combined with being attractive and exhibiting heterosexual appeal—the "heterosexy athlete"—form the primary markers signifying dominant adolescent femininity (see, in particular, Adams, Schmitke, and

Franklin 2005; Bettis and Adams 2005). Thus, feminine social hierarchies develop in relation to body type and bodily behavior, such somatic differentiation affirms inequality among girls, and diverse femininities are constructed in relation to bodily development. And Kristen reported finding herself embedded in such a hierarchy, which clearly suggests that future research examine inequalities among girls. Indeed, this is especially important for analysis of crime that takes place in institutions like schools as well as in peer groups and gangs.

Moreover, what the above additionally demonstrates is that dominant femininity in these settings is not established simply through the display of certain types of bodies and bodily behaviors—such as tall, slim, and sporty—but also through distancing oneself from different subordinate forms of embodiment. And one way to accomplish such distancing is by bullying "Other" girls, a practice that situates one's feminine embodiment as "superior" to "inferior" embodied feminine displays/behaviors. Not surprisingly, previous research supports the conclusion that dominant femininity regularly is constructed through the bullying of subordinate femininities (Brown 2003; Faris and Felmlee 2011; Merten 1997; Owens and Duncan 2009). Popular girls often sustain a positive self-concept through their ability to assert bullying power over "Other" girls, and they are able to bully without censure because victims normally are hesitant to challenge their power (Crothers, Field, and Kolbert 2005; Rose, Swenson, and Waller 2004). Thus, the ability to bully is a form of power whereby "popular" girls command and control interaction among girls, exercising a dominant position by policing the boundaries of acceptable femininity and simultaneously demarcating subordinate delegitimated femininities, such as those practiced by Kristen. This information consequently powerfully points to future research attending to how dominant femininities are constructed in differing social situations, and how those dominant femininities are different from other dominant femininities as well as emphasized, subordinate, and equality femininities.

The importance of corporeal difference and bullying power notwithstanding, Kristen's life story also underlines that dominant femininities—like dominant masculinities—are supported through constructs of heterosexuality. As the data in chapters 3, 4, and 5 show, adolescence is a time in life when agency and body become connected to sexuality and to "do" heterosexuality is an everyday dominant feminine (and masculine) bodily practice, such sexual orientation being an important source of acceptable feminine (and masculine) identity. Particularly within female group "sex talk," however, sexuality is not represented simply as "being heterosexual"; one must not be excessively active ("slut" or "loose") or unreasonably inactive ("virgin" or "cock teaser") heterosexually. This of course is associated with the culturally constructed "male sexual drive" discourse discussed above, as Gavey (2005: 105) explains:

> Of course it is possible for women to resist the male sexual drive discourse, but for heterosexual women this can never be a matter of stepping outside of it without the possibility of being marked by it. For example, within our culture the woman who chooses to not have sex with her male partner when she doesn't feel like it herself enters a discursive space spiked with pejorative and potentially punitive consequences [cock teaser]. . . . There is a whole other set of discursive resources available for punishing and policing a woman whose sexuality is deemed excessive [slut]. . . . These kinds of accusations—about both sexual excess and sexual insufficiency—are not trivial. They enter the social with effect.

And of course such verbal bullying had a profound impact on Kristen whereby she was *doubly* subordinated as sexually excessive (slut) and sexually insufficient (peewee virgin) by different groups of girls. It thus seems that such sexual bullying—and its relation to the "male sexual drive" discourse—should be prominent in future feminist research, in both criminology and sociology.

One of the consequences of the above verbal bullying, and as is shown in Kristen's life story, is that adolescent girls (and boys) construct different and unequal notions of heterosexuality to establish hierarchies among them. Although heterosexuality is exalted throughout adolescent culture, girls categorized as heterosexual and sexually excessive or sexually insufficient are publicly represented by the popular dominant girls as demonstrating a subordinate heterosexuality and thereby a subordinate femininity. Indeed, within the social settings in which Kristen participated, certain notions of other-sex sex, desire, and relationships were celebrated and privileged and, thus, dominant femininities were heterosexualized. Consequently, one way to validate dominant femininity is to express and define oneself as practicing a specific type of heterosexuality both by demeaning subordinate heterosexualities and by engaging in moderately active heterosexual practices and "sex talk."[3]

Although the dominant heterofemininity in school—characterized by slim, tall, and sporty/athletic bodies bullying "Other" subordinate heterofemininities, and practicing a specific type of heterosexuality (moderately active)—is associated with the "prep/jock" girls in Kristen's life story, some of these bodily displays and practices are current, common, celebrated, and omnipresent within adolescent-girl culture generally, crossing all girl-clique boundaries in this study, such as those constructed by the "chicks." Despite the fact that these latter girls were deemed subordinate by the "prep/jocks" as "sluts," the "chicks" contextually constructed their own form of dominant femininity: overweight yet inordinately feminine, "forward," excessively practiced heterosexuality, and bullying heterosexually inactive "virgins" were acceptable feminine practices. Thus, a variety of dominant heterofemininities exist within adolescent-girl culture, each of which is situationally constructed differently and, depending upon the social setting, certain heterofemininities are more powerful and privileged (dominant) than alternative (subordinate) forms of heterofemininities. Future research on the inequalities among heterofemininities (as well as heteromasculinities) will thus be invaluable; indeed, the entire area of "sexualities" and their relation to "sex" and "gender" as well as to crime and violence is vitally important to the future of criminological and sociological scholarship.[4]

A Girl Sex Offender?

It is estimated that between approximately 15 and 20 percent of all sexual offenses are committed by people under the age of eighteen, that approximately 90 percent of these offenses are committed by adolescent boys and 10 percent by adolescent girls, and that many adult sexual offenders began their offending as youth (Gannon and Cortoni 2010; Vick, McRoy, and Matthews 2002; Zolondek, Abel, Northey, and Jordan 2003). Until recently, social scientists paid scant attention to sexual offenses committed by adolescent girls, the research to date having concentrated on identifying and describing characteristics that *may* correlate with such offending (Schwartz, Cavanaugh, Pimental, and Prentky 2006; Vick, McRoy, and Matthews 2002). For example, previous research has found that the majority of girl offenders frequently (1) victimize children who are much younger; (2) come from "dysfunctional families" (e.g., where often they are the victims of some combination of physical, sexual, and emotional abuse); and (3) exhibit problems (issues) with peer relationships (Gannon and Cortoni 2010; Righthand and Welch 2005). However, it remains unclear how, and to what extent, these dynamics actually influence the development of adolescent sexual offenses by girls. Causal relationships are difficult to establish because of possible mediating factors not yet identified, possible variable interaction among characteristics already identified, and other variables as to how each characteristic may or may not contribute to sexual offending. In other words, simple correlation does not merit causal influence. For example, many more girls than boys are sexually victimized within the family, yet the vast majority of adolescent sexual offenders are boys. Moreover, the identified terms "girl" and "sexual" in the label "adolescent-girl sexual offenders" triggers a second major concern with earlier research: because studies of adolescent sexual offending by girls are appallingly gender and sexuality blind, no previous research considered the impact of both gender and sexuality on these girls. Historically, then, the gendered and sexual adolescent-girl sexual offender remained missing from this research and, therefore, studies did not consider the salient relationship among the social construction of sex, gender, sexuality, and such offending.

My interview with Kristen has sought to help remedy these crucial oversights. In chapter 4 I scrutinized Kristen's movement from having been bullied to engaging specifically in reactive outside-school sexual offenses. I also outlined numerous simi-

larities between Sam and Kristen and their eventual sexual offending: both were the victims of continuous bullying; they both
entered into reflexivity to internally decide how best to solve
their oppressive dilemma; and they both engaged in sexual offending in an attempt to invalidate their "deviant heterogender"
label and become recognized as a "heterogender conformist."

Nevertheless, there are important differences between Sam
and Kristen that are related to heteromasculinity and heterofemininity. First, and as discussed above, embedded in Sam's
narrative is an adherence to the "male sexual drive" discourse
as he reflexively resolved that he is *entitled* to heterosexuality
when he wants it and he is *entitled* to apply manipulative pressure on young girls to convince them to provide him with the
sexual pleasure he desires. However, no such explicit reference
to entitlement exists in Kristen's life story; in fact, Kristen indicated her primary motive was to simply "try sex" so as to see if
she could "have sex like 'the chicks.'" Nevertheless, second, we
do see in Kristen's interviews conformity to the "male sexual
drive" discourse in the sense that in her school, dominant heterofeminine bodily displays and behaviors considered acceptable
by both adolescent boys and girls are those that primarily serve
the sexual interest of boys. And in the differing in-school social
settings within which Kristen participated, dominant heterofemininities stipulated that girls must fashion their body as a sexual
object principally to attract the attention of boys, and that any
eventual sexual practices are intended primarily to satisfy boys'
sexual desires. Indeed, both Sam and Kristen gained knowledge
through interaction at school as to what sexuality is—heterosexuality—and they both learned who does what sexually to
whom and how; for example, girls give "hand jobs" and "blow
jobs" to boys. Thus, for Kristen, although heterosexuality was
a *salient* feature of her sense of self, she constructed her sexual
violence in such a way that concentrated on "trying sex" through
fondling rather than striving to realize her own sexual pleasure
through sexual violence. Recall Kristen's statement: "He seemed
to like it and I liked that." Kristen now felt like a "chick" "'cause
I'm doing what they brag about." In contrast, for Sam heterosexuality likewise was a *salient* feature of his sense of self, yet he

constructed his sexual violence in such a way that the girls he babysat were manipulatively coerced to generate sexual pleasure for him. Thus, the juxtaposition of Kristen and Sam reveals how the "male sexual drive" discourse differently impacts each, and clearly much more research is obviously needed on this differing impact on boys and girls and their eventual involvement in sexual violence.[5] Third, Sam purposely scared the girls he babysat by wrestling with them, as he would "throw them around" and "make it look like I was invincible, like I was strong, tough, and couldn't be hurt." Differing from Sam, Kristen approached the seven-year-old boy in such a way that he would feel "okay" with her and that he would "not be scared." Fourth, Sam engaged in sexual violence in part for power and control, which were practiced through his ability to "trap" the girls he babysat so that "they didn't have much of a choice but to go along with what I wanted them to do." For Kristen, power and control were not initial motives; however, power and control were embedded in the meaning of the sexually violent interaction and, resultantly, were an unexpected added bonus: "I like decided what to do and that felt good, you know, 'cause I never had that either." Finally, Sam's victims initially said "no" to his sexual advances yet, as he states, "I like bugged them and bugged them until they didn't say no." In contrast, the boy Kristen victimized did not resist but in fact "kept lying on the grass and closed his eyes. It was like he really liked it. He didn't say anything or fight me, so I just kept doing it." Furthermore, the boy met Kristen at the park again twice and they did "the same thing." The comparison then of Sam and Kristen alerts us to the question of consent—the girls clearly did not consent to Sam (and he practiced heteromasculinity by prevailing over their resistance) yet did the boy actually consent to Kristen? Although in both cases age of consent laws clearly were violated, the case of Kristen suggests a distinct heterofeminine reading whereby the "perpetrator-victim" relationship seemingly allowed for the "victim" to comply willingly and not conceptualize the interaction as abusive.[6]

Arguably, then, there exist important embodied *gender* differences in the sexual violence committed by Sam and Kristen. And it is crucially important that future research address such differences (and similarities), yet such a research program involves first acknowledging that girls/women can and do engage in sexual violence against boys/men—although irrefutably not equally in terms of frequency and severity. A significant limitation of previous feminist sexual violence research that solely investigates the dichotomy of boys'/men's sexual *violence* and girls'/women's sexual *victimization* "is that it reifies understandings of women's sexuality as passive, submissive, and vulnerable, and men's as active, aggressive, and dangerous. In doing so it arguably risks contributing to discourses/knowledge that actually perpetuate the very dynamic of rigidly gendered heterosex that arguably supports the rape and sexual coercion of women" (Gavey 2005: 196). I agree with Gavey (194) that it is vitally important to research girls and women acting in a sexually violent way toward boys and men because by doing so it will create the space "to seriously disrupt the dominant discourses of heterosexuality that cast women as passive and men as active," and it therefore has a "radical potential for a feminist analysis of rape and sexual coercion (of women, by men)."

The comparison of Sam and Kristen then suggests dissimilarity in the meanings and eventual configurations of their individual forms of sexual violence, which at once are embedded in, and drawn from, the everyday heteromasculine/feminine scripts practiced at school. Accordingly, more research is needed concentrating on the relationship between the contextual social construction of heterosexuality and how such situational interaction impacts subsequent sexual violence by certain boys and girls. There is a substantial need for comparative studies of boys and girls as well as research concentrating distinctly on girls/women's involvement in sexual violence. Nevertheless, research *must* also simultaneously continue to examine the unquestionably much more widespread, threatening, and harmful forms of sexual violence committed by boys/men against girls/women.

The Salience of Home *and* School

As noted in chapters 3 and 4, for the four sexual and assaultive youth, the culture of the school and conversations with parents at home both defined "fighting back" as *the* proper response to bullying. However, for Jerry and Karen, a different relationship between home and school was prevalent. Nevertheless, Jerry's life story is different from Karen's and all of the violent adolescents, so I begin this section with a discussion of that distinction. Following this I examine specifically how Jerry and Karen are similar and different, while concurrently contrasting Jerry and Karen with the four violent adolescents in this study.

Jerry's life story demonstrates that an acceptance of assaultive violence as a means of responding to bullying may develop exclusively outside the home. The bullying Jerry experienced on the playground, as well as his interactions with others in that setting, gave rise to Jerry's conception of what the appropriate masculine means are for managing such "playground business." If Jerry chose not to bully or fight back, his masculinity would remain subordinated. Consequently, in order for him to avoid this "inferior" status he would have to "bring somebody else down." Thus for Jerry it was the playground milieu that offered "fighting back" to provocation as a suitable resource for "doing masculinity"—a violent response to threat was defined in that setting as the contextually appropriate masculine practice for overcoming the challenge. The cultural ideals of what it meant to be a "real man" on Jerry's playground encouraged a specific line of social action. And Jerry actively appropriated and then applied that ideal to the masculinity challenges he faced. Jerry drew on existing forms of social action to construct a particular masculinity for the specific setting of the playground. Accordingly, in third grade Jerry developed a masculine project—prior to discussing the issue with his parents—that entailed responding to masculinity challenges through violence. Interaction on the playground—not at home—first motivated Jerry toward violence, providing a resource for affirming a particular type of masculinity.

Despite the above, interaction between Jerry and his parents, and Karen and her mother, shaped a different relationship to violence than such interaction did for Lenny, Kelly, Sam, and Kristen. For Jerry, he received contradictory signals. On the one hand, the culture of the school suggested "fighting back"; on the other hand, his parents encouraged "walking away." Thus both the home and the school offered Jerry different approaches for responding to interpersonal problems at school, and the construction of both violent and nonviolent masculinities resulted from interplay between family and school. For Lenny, Kelly, and Sam, through interaction at school and at home, primarily with their stepfather/father, all three subsequently and reflexively decided that being masculine meant initially responding to provocation with assaultive violence. The life history of Jerry is similar yet significantly different from these three violent youths. Jerry was bullied often by peers at school for his physical shape and for not being "a man." Although Jerry first responded through violence, he continued to feel insecure and "small inside." Consequently, he felt extremely distressed over continued bullying victimization at school. However, in Jerry's discussion with his parents about the disturbing masculine situation at school, his parents responded to his concerns, they attempted to understand his plight, and they underscored that it was wholly inappropriate for Jerry to respond to any type of provocation with violence. Jerry experienced a warm and affectionate relationship with his parents, who demonstrated that care in supportive and harmonious ways, and they never blamed him for any of the family problems he experienced at home. Because Jerry had developed such a close and mutually respectful relationship with his parents, he accepted their opinions on the appropriate response to bullying at school. In other words, he felt confident to "walk away." Indeed, such social action represents self-confidence rather than self-doubt, and this is a completely different relationship with parents than Lenny, Kelly, and Sam experienced.

For Karen, she did not receive contradictory signals from home and school, as there is no indication in her narrative of girl victims of bullying at school being encouraged by co-present interactants to "fight back" against the bullies. Similarly, Kristen does not report observing girls "fighting back" when bullied by other girls at school. However, Kristen's mother did suggest to her that if someone verbally bullies her she should simply "walk away," but if she is consistently verbally and/or physically bullied at school, she should "hit them for it." Karen's experience at home is different. Like Kristen, Karen was consistently verbally bullied for her size and shape at school, yet in contrast to Kristen, Karen was able to discuss in depth with her mother this distressing feminine situation at school. Like Jerry's parents, Karen's mother responded to her oppressive situation at school, attempted to understand Karen's predicament, and never suggested that Karen respond through assaultive violence. Karen experienced a devoted, affectionate, and loving relationship with her mother, who was always supportive. Karen's mother talked with the school principal and when this failed to curb the bullying, she implemented "Plan B," involving both Karen and herself exercising and dieting *together*. Thus, this close interaction between mother and daughter at home helped nullify any need for a physical or verbal response to the bullies at school.

Additionally, and once again in contrast to Lenny, Kelly, Sam, and Kristen, Jerry experienced several relationships and social circumstances at school that helped bolster his turn to nonviolence. First, the method of "walking away," as stated, "worked." When he refused to acknowledge the bullies by simply ignoring their actions and going about his own business, the bullying seemed to diminish over time. Second, Jerry developed close relationships with other youth who deemphasized the importance of the body to one's sense of self-worth. These youth accepted Jerry's body "as is," so that dominant masculine body images and practices were not essential criteria to their friends for "doing masculinity." Thus, for Jerry, his body mediated and influenced his social action and directed him toward friends who accepted his body. Finally, Jerry's friends eschewed any use of violence to solve interpersonal problems—they were the "laid-back" group in school. Indeed, Jerry, like Kelly (although in a different way), *disrupts* gender *and* sexual difference through his nonviolent, celibate, and laid-back equality masculinity.

Jerry's life history also differs specifically from Sam's in an important respect. Although Sam and Jerry both recounted their adoption of heterosexuality at school, Sam alone developed a feeling of entitlement to heterosexuality when he wanted it. Sam did not discuss sexuality with any adult, he was unable to engage in heterosexual dating, and he formed no friendships with girls. Jerry's relationship to heterosexuality was quite different. He openly discussed sexuality with his parents; he had relatives and friends who were gay; his parents emphasized that they did not care what his sexual orientation was; and he had two girlfriends in junior high school. Although Jerry identified as heterosexual and remained a "virgin" in high school, he had numerous girl *friends* with whom he spent time; engaging in sexuality was not something he had to do "right now," and there was no indication he felt entitled to heterosexuality. Thus, these particular forms of interaction at home *and* at school that Jerry experienced kept sexuality as a bodily masculine practice from becoming the obsession it was for Sam. Indeed, for Jerry, and like Lenny, *the "male sexual drive" was not a salient feature in his reflexivity and sense of self.*

Karen, in contrast to Lenny, Kelly, Sam, and Kristen, experienced new developments in her interaction with her mother and new relationships at school, both of which helped sustain her nonviolence. First, because of the exercise and diet program with her mother, Karen lost twenty pounds, which had a major impact on her size and shape. Second, Karen joined the high school swim team and after being verbally bullied by an ex-classmate from middle school, a challenge to race the bully was organized by a swim-team friend. Karen agreed to participate in the race and she won, which had the effect of bolstering her feminine self-confidence. Third, Karen developed close relationships with, in particular, boys and girls on the swim team, who exclusively made positive comments about Karen's body. In short, Karen's body now "fit in" with the popular feminine body images and practices at school—she became a dominant and nonviolent "heterosexy athlete."

Karen's life history also differs from Kristen's in an important respect. Kristen developed an obsession with "trying sex" and engaging in sex like the "chicks," yet she was unable to participate in heterosexual dating, she formed no close friendships with boys or girls, and she did not discuss sexuality with any adult. Karen's relationship to sexuality was quite different, as she openly discussed sexuality with her mother, who helped her obtain birth-control pills; she began to date boys and eventually engaged in intercourse for the first time; she developed close friendships with girls and was a frequent participant in the heterofeminine girl "sex talk" at school; and every weekend she joined with other boys and girls "to party." Thus, these particular forms of interaction at home and at school kept sexuality as a bodily feminine practice from becoming the fixation it was for Kristen.

The differing interplay between home and school created a setting for the social construction of violent and nonviolent heteromasculinities/femininities. The life stories show that the boys and girls in this study resolved bullying situations at school in ways related to differing interactions at home and school. As the boys and girls went back and forth from home to school, the practices they constructed in school were reoriented around what resulted from interaction at home; conversely, their practices at home (e.g., discussing or refusing to discuss the bullying) were altered based on interaction at school. The interrelatedness of home and school, and the reflexive choices made by all six adolescents during the interchange, resulted in the social construction of violence or nonviolence by adolescent boys and girls. And this data suggest the need for much more scholarly work on the relation between home and school and how that relationship impacts violence and nonviolence.

Moreover, the particular life stories of Kelly, Kristen, and Karen add to the abundant research on girl's *pathways* into violence and nonviolence, as the most common pathway to girls' involvement in crime is physical and/or sexual victimization in the family (Chesney-Lind and Pasko 2004). There is no evidence that Kelly, Kristen, or Karen were the victims of physical or sexual violence at home, although Kelly did witness severe violence by her stepfather against her mother and sisters, and Kristen was the victim of verbal abuse by her stepfather. Nevertheless, it seems that a significant pathway factor for both Kelly and Kristen was their relationship with a particular parent—stepfather and mother respectively—and the parental encouragement of solving the bullying victimization problem through violence, that is, "fighting back." Karen's mother, however, conceived nonviolent solutions to her victimization, such as talking with the principal and participating with Karen in a dieting and exercising program. Consequently, and not to minimize the significance of physical and sexual violence in girls' pathways to crime, the life stories of Kelly, Kristen, and Karen suggest that future pathways research on the nature of girls' overall relationship with parents/guardians, and how that relationship is associated with interaction at school, would be beneficial.

Social Policies

In closing, let me briefly suggest several salient social policies for curbing bullying in school and its eventual reactive violence. First, a critical policy concern of the immediate future is managing gender and sexual relations and the widespread bullying they produce. Such a policy must concentrate on the relationship among bullying, violence, and embodied (hetero)masculinities/femininities. At the least, secondary schools should publish and widely distribute to students, parents, teachers, and town officials a "school policy statement" which emphasizes that the entire community will not tolerate the bullying of one student by another and that the school endorses an alternative interactional climate based on respecting diversity, thereby critically challenging bullying and its accompanied power within the school (Salisbury and Jackson 1996). The school policy statement should also disclose that most forms of bullying fall under the provisions of Title IX that prohibit discrimination on the basis of "sex." Title IX is violated if the bullying creates a hostile environment—for example, if the student's ability to participate in or benefit from programs and activities offered at school are limited or hindered by the bullying (Ali 2010). Two forms of bullying covered under Title IX are *sexual harassment* and *gender-based harassment*: the former includes calling students sexually charged names, spreading sexual rumors, and rating students on sexual activity or performance; the latter involves verbally indicating that a student has "failed" to conform to dominant notions of masculinity and femininity (6–8). Importantly, Title IX prohibits these forms of bullying regardless of the "sex" of the bully; that is, even if the bully and the victim are of the same "sex," a violation has occurred. Thus, the school policy statement should include all of the relevant Title IX information as well as indicating that school officials both expect the reporting of all bullying incidents (by bystanders as well as victims) and that they will fulfill their obligations under Title IX to take immediate and effective action to eliminate the bullying and thus the hostile environment. Finally, one approach to highlight the school policy statement would involve developing mandatory school sessions in which students and teachers explore situations when students do *not* act in accordance with bullying and (hetero)masculine/feminine power relations. This creates time for students to discuss how and when to act in a courageous, caring, and valuing way to challenge the gender and sexuality dominant messages in the school (Denborough 1996).

Second, the school curriculum should be scrutinized to create both gender/sexuality-specific and gender/sexuality-relevant strategies, such as making gender *and* sexual relations a core subject in public schools (gender/sexuality relevant) and creating personal-development programs that are specifically designed for boys and for girls of all sexual orientations (gender/sexuality specific). Such a curriculum will help address gender/sexual hierarchies and bullying by including topics such as interpersonal gender/sexual violence; conflict resolution and alternative nonviolent responses to bullying; sex/gender/sexuality awareness; and valuing the diversity of masculinities, femininities, and sexualities (Connell 1996).

Finally, schools should pursue an explicit goal of social justice because certain practices in schools—such as bullying—perpetuate injustice, and therefore pursuing social justice requires addressing gender and sexual patterns that support these practices (Connell 1996). Arguably, developing programs in schools that challenge division and inequality and emphasize empathy and acceptance of diversity are essential. Building such issues into the curriculum enables a school to begin challenging the notion of "Other" and to organize knowledge based on inclusion of the least advantaged in terms of gender and sexuality. Such a policy reconfigures knowledge to open up the possibilities that current social inequalities conceal, demanding a capacity for empathy/diversity and thus taking the viewpoint of the other (Connell 1995).

These suggested policies—school policy statements, gender/sexuality-relevant and gender/sexuality-specific curriculum, and emphasis on social justice and empathy and pluralism in schools—obviously neither exhaustive nor comprehensive[7]—argue persuasively that the topic of embodied heterogender is highly relevant to debates on bullying and eventual violent offending by victims. What these policies essentially aim to do is "re-embody" youth by allowing them to recognize alternative and different ways of acting in and through their body, thereby helping to develop embodied capacities other than those associated with bullying and interpersonal violence.

Notes

Chapter 1: Introduction

1. Cesare Lombroso (1835–1909) was the preeminent nineteenth-century biological criminologist who employed anthropometry in an attempt to make known the alleged "dangers" to society by uncovering *the* "criminal body." For a contemporary critique of Lombroso, see Horn (2003) and Messerschmidt (2004). In addition to Lombroso, Sutherland (1947) also devoted much time to criticizing the "body type" theorists, such as Hooton (1939a, b) and Sheldon (1949).

2. It must be noted, however, that Sutherland discussed (albeit briefly) how criminal acts are practices by embodied people in co-present interactions. For example, Sutherland (1924: 180; 1947: 93) consistently argued in his textbook that certain youth with "physiological defects"—such as crossed eyes or an unusually small or large body—may be ridiculed at school, eventually ostracized by law-abiding groups, and thereby "forced into" association with "anti-social groups." Thus, Sutherland not only rejected any notion of criminal acts as preprogrammed in the bodies of individual offenders, he also hinted at some youthful offenders being motivated to engage in crime through experiences with their bodies and through the way their bodies were received and treated by peers. Nevertheless, Sutherland never formally included agency as embodied interaction in differential association theory and, thus, clearly became the most influential figure in inaugurating a disembodied, dualist, sociological criminology.

3. Some sociological criminologists have integrated biology into their theoretical frameworks, but not *embodiment* or the *lived body* as a necessary and mediate component of social action. For example, in both social control (Hirschi 1969) and self-control (Gottfredson and Hirschi 1990) theories, there is a built-in assumption that antisocial tendencies are naturalized in the body and actualized only if various sorts of social control are relaxed or the individual does not learn self-control. These "control" ideas appear rooted in Christian notions that view the body as naturally sinful and in need of strict regulation by the mind.

4. My book *Masculinities and Crime* (1993) likewise can be criticized for contributing to both a disembodied and gender difference approach, as it completely ignores the body as well as the fact that girls and women sometimes engage in masculine practices and "male crime."

5. See Cealey Harrison and Hood-Williams' (2002) important book *Beyond Sex and Gender* for an excellent extended discussion of this question.

Chapter 2: Theory and Method

1. Sexuality involves all erotic and nonerotic aspects of social life and social being that relate to bodily attraction or intimate bodily contact between individuals, such as desires, practices, discourses, interactions, relationships, and identities (see Jackson and Scott 2010).

2. The method is a modified version of Jean-Paul Sartre's "existential psychoanalysis." For further discussion of existential psychoanalysis, see Sartre (1956: 712–34) and Connell (1987: 211–17).

3. Because of the in-depth and complex quality of the interviews, in chapters 3, 4, and 5 I report only *six* of the thirty life stories. In the overall sample of assaultive offenders (ten), sexual offenders (ten), and nonviolent youth (ten), I rejected only one interview (a male sexual offender) because of continual inconsistencies (I learned later this interviewee was severely medicated) and another interview because the boy (also a sexual offender) was unable to discuss further his past relationship with his father (he broke down crying). The remaining twenty-four interviews of boys and girls are not reported in this book because of what is referred to in the literature as a "saturation-of-information" effect (Seidman 1998: 48). In other words, during the data analysis I reached a point where I began to find strikingly similar types of information being reported—I was no longer hearing anything "new." Therefore, these twenty-four stories are additionally not part of the discussion because they added nothing new to the data

and would have produced only repetition. Moreover, I do not discuss how the boys and girls were caught nor the resolution of their cases, as this information could reveal their identity. Finally, my selection of white working-class boys and girls limits any generalization to racial-minority working-class youth as well as to middle-class youth. Clearly, there is a need for life-history research on these latter two categories of boys and girls.

Chapter 6: Conclusion

1. The discursive notion of a natural "male sexual drive" is relatively recent, as for most of Western history men were extolled for their proficiency at resisting sexual temptations because engagement in excessive sexuality was thought to weaken and emasculate men. For example, although considering sexuality instinctual, in the late fifteenth century a man who "indulged in excessive eating, drinking, sleeping, or sex—who failed to 'rule himself'—was considered unfit to rule his household, much less polity" (Lipton 2011: A35; see also, Neal 2008 and Dunlop 2007). Around the nineteenth century, the alleged natural "male sexual drive" emerged; women lacked such a drive, yet the view was that they did have the "potential for desire that could be activated by the sexual advances of a man" (Jackson and Scott 2010: 59). And this nineteenth-century construction of the "male sexual drive" socially "positioned it as the core of masculinity and of man's essential self" (59).

2. The "dyke" label attached to Kelly by the dominant feminine girls in her school was assigned to her for not "properly" constructing heterofemininity and thus in the process negatively disparaged same-sex sexuality among girls.

3. Arguably "sex talk"—which all six adolescents in this study either participated in or wanted to partake in but were excluded from—is an example of a nonerotic form of "doing heterosexuality" in which heterosexuals regularly and publicly express their heterosexual identity through talk. For example, in an important study, Celia Kitzinger (2005b) found that heterosexuals reproduce "in their talk a normative taken-for-granted heterosexual world. . . . [T]he *public* identities they display in interaction are insistently heterosexual—and over the course of the interactions in which they are engaged, these co-conversationalists reflect and reproduce a profoundly heteronormative social order." Thus, heteronormativity is reproduced in ordinary, everyday forms of

"sex talk," and each of the six interviewees routinely encountered such talk at school.

4. For an excellent discussion of femininities, see the important new book by Charlebois 2011.

5. In the history of heterosexuality, the persistence of feminine sexual passivity has gradually eroded so that today the emphasis is on women as active rather than merely responsive partners (Jackson and Scott 2010). And for adolescents in particular, the age of first intercourse has declined for both boys and girls yet the rate for "virginity" has declined more rapidly for girls, and the number of teenagers who have had more than five sexual partners by age eighteen has increased for both boys and girls, yet the rate of increase for girls is greater (Kimmel 2005). And according to Kristen, in her school being sexually "active" seems to necessitate primarily satisfying the sexual desires of boys and such "active" sexuality is imperative to retaining a relationship with both boys *and* girls.

6. There is the strong possibility that the boy was too young to have "access to the sexual scripts through which acts, relationships and feelings (emotions and sensations) become sexually meaningful" (Jackson and Scott, 2010: 113) and, therefore, he conceptualized Kristen as simply engaging in caressing and nurturing behavior. I thank Lisa Arellano for discussing with me—and offering much insight on—the "girl perpetrator–boy victim" relationship in such cases.

7. See Klein 2011 for a more comprehensive discussion of anti-bullying policies for secondary schools.

References

Adams, N., A. Schmitke, and A. Franklin. 2005. "Tomboys, Dykes, and Girly Girls: Interrogating the Subjectivities of Adolescent Female Athletes." *Women's Studies Quarterly* 33 (1/2): 73–91.

Agnew, R. 1990. "The Origins of Delinquent Events: An Examination of Offender Accounts." *Journal of Research in Crime and Delinquency* 27 (3): 267–94.

Ali, R. 2010. "Dear Colleague Letter: Harassment and Bullying." United States Department of Education, Office of Civil Rights. (October 26): 1–10.

Allen, J. 1989. "Men, Crime, and Criminology: Recasting the Questions." *International Journal of the Sociology of Law* 17 (1): 19–39.

Andersen, M. L. 1993. "Studying across Difference: Race, Class, and Gender in Qualitative Research." In J. H. Stanfield and R. M. Dennis, eds. *Race and Ethnicity in Research Methods*, 39–52. Newbury Park, CA: Sage.

Archer, M. 2007. *Making Our Way through the World: Human Reflexivity and Social Mobility*. New York: Cambridge University Press.

Beasley, C. 2008. "Rethinking Hegemonic Masculinity in a Globalizing World." *Men and Masculinities* 11 (1): 86–103.

Belknap, J. 2006. *The Invisible Woman: Gender, Crime, and Justice*. Belmont, CA: Wadsworth.

Bettis, P., and N. Adams, eds. 2005. *Geographies of Girlhood: Identities In-Between*. Mahwah, NJ: Lawrence Erlbaum.

Bowker, L., ed. 1998. *Masculinities and Violence*. Thousand Oaks, CA: Sage.

Britton, D. 2011. *The Gender of Crime*. Lanham, MD: Rowman & Littlefield.

Brown, L. M. 2003. *Girlfighting: Betrayal and Rejection among Girls*. New York: New York University Press.

Burman, M., S. Batchelor, and J. Brown. 2001. "Researching Girls and Violence: Facing the Dilemmas of Fieldwork." *British Journal of Criminology* 41 (3): 443–59.

Carlen, P., and T. Jefferson. 1996. *British Journal of Criminology, Special Issue, Masculinities and Crime* 33 (6).

Cealey Harrison, W. 2006. "The Shadow and the Substance: The Sex / Gender Debate." In K. Davis, M. Evans, and J. Lorber, eds. *Handbook of Gender and Women's Studies*, 35–52. Thousand Oaks, CA: Sage.

Cealey Harrison, W., and J. Hood-Williams. 2002. *Beyond Sex and Gender*. Thousand Oaks, CA: Sage.

Chambliss, W. 1972. *The Box Man: A Professional Thief's Journey*. New York: Harper & Row.

Charlebois, J. 2011. *Gender and the Construction of Dominant, Hegemonic, and Oppositional Femininities*. Lanham, MD: Rowman & Littlefield.

Chesney-Lind, M., and K. Irwin. 2007. *Beyond Bad Girls: Gender, Violence, and Hype*. New York: Routledge.

Chesney-Lind, M., and N. Jones. 2010. *Fighting for Girls: New Perspectives on Gender and Violence*. Albany: SUNY Press.

Chesney-Lind, M., and L. Pasko. 2004. *The Female Offender: Girls, Women, and Crime*. 2nd ed. Thousand Oaks, CA: Sage.

Collier, R. 1998. *Masculinities, Crime and Criminology: Men, Heterosexuality and the Criminal(ised) Other*. London: Sage.

Connell, R. 2000. *The Men and the Boys*. Sydney: Allen & Unwin.

———. 1998. "Making Gendered People: Bodies, Identities, Sexualities." In M. M. Ferree, J. Lorber, and B. B. Hess, eds. *Revisioning Gender*, 449–71. Thousand Oaks, CA: Sage.

———. 1997. "Why is Classical Theory Classical?" *American Journal of Sociology* 102 (6): 1511–57.

———. 1996. "Teaching the Boys: New Research on Masculinity and Gender Strategies for Schools." *Teachers College Record* 98 (2): 206–35.

———. 1995. *Masculinities*. Berkeley: University of California Press.

———. 1991. "Live Fast and Die Young: The Construction of Masculinity among Young Working-Class Men on the Margin of the Labour Market." *Australian and New Zealand Journal of Sociology* 27 (2): 141–71.

———. 1987. *Gender and Power: Society, the Person, and Sexual Politics*. Stanford: Stanford University Press.

Connell, R., and J. W. Messerschmidt. 2005. "Hegemonic Masculinity: Rethinking the Concept." *Gender & Society* 19 (6): 829–59.

Crawley, S. L., L. J. Foley, and C. L. Shehan. 2008. *Gendering Bodies.* Lanham, MD: Rowman & Littlefield.

Crossley, N. 2006. *Reflexive Embodiment in Contemporary Society.* New York: Open University Press.

Crossley, N. 2001. *The Social Body: Habit, Identity and Desire.* Thousand Oaks, CA: Sage.

———. 1995. "Body Techniques, Agency and Intercorporeality: On Goffman's *Relations in Public,*" *Sociology* 29 (1): 133–49.

Crothers, L. M., J. E. Field, and J. B. Kolbert. 2005. "Navigating Power, Control, and Being Nice: Aggression and Adolescent Girls' Friendships." *Journal of Counseling and Development* 83 (3): 349–54.

Daly, K., and M. Chesney-Lind. 1988. "Feminism and Criminology." *Justice Quarterly* 5 (4): 497–538.

Daly, K., and L. Maher, eds. 1998. *Criminology at the Crossroads: Feminist Readings in Crime and Justice.* New York: Oxford University Press.

Davis, K. 1997. "Embody-ing Theory: Beyond Modernist and Postmodernist Readings of the Body." In K. Davis, ed. *Embodied Practices: Feminist Perspectives on the Body,* 1–23. Thousand Oaks, CA: Sage.

Davis, S., and C. Nixon. 2010. *The Youth Voice Project.* Available at: youthvoiceproject.com.

de Beauvoir, S. (1949) 1972. *The Second Sex.* New York: Penguin.

Denborough, D. 1996. "Step by Step: Developing Respectful and Effective Ways of Working with Young Men to Reduce Violence." In C. McLean, M. Carey, and C. White, eds. *Men's Ways of Being,* 91–115. Boulder, CO: Westview.

Dowsett, G. W. 1996. *Practicing Desire: Homosexual Sex in the Era of Aids.* Stanford, CA: Stanford University Press.

Dunlop, F. S. 2007. *The Late Medieval Interlude: The Drama of Youth and Aristocratic Masculinity.* Woodbridge, UK: York Medieval Press.

Ekins, R., and D. King. 2006. *The Transgender Phenomenon.* Thousand Oaks, CA: Sage.

Ellis, H. 1897. *Sexual Inversion.* New York: Palgrave.

Engels, F. 1970. *The Origin of the Family, Private Property, and the State.* New York: Pathfinder Press.

Erling, A., and P. Hwang. 2004. "Swedish 10-Year-Old Children's Perceptions and Experiences of Bullying." *Journal of School Violence* 3: 33–43.

Faris, R., and D. Felmlee. 2011. "Social Struggles: Network Centrality and Gender Segregation in Same- and Cross-Gender Aggression." *American Sociological Review* 76 (1): 48–73.

Foucault, M. 1980. *Herculine Barbin.* New York: Vintage.

Frisen, A., A. Jonsson, and C. Persson. 2007. "Adolescents' Perception of Bullying: Who Is the Victim? Who Is the Bully? What Can Be Done to Stop Bullying?" *Adolescence* 42: 749–61.

Galliher, J. F., and C. Tyree. 1985. "Edwin Sutherland's Research on the Origin of Sexual Psychopath Laws: An Early Case Study of the Medicalization of Deviance." *Social Problems* 33 (2): 100–113.

Gannon, T. A., and F. Cortoni, eds. 2010. *Female Sexual Offenders: Theory, Assessment and Treatment.* Malden, MA: Wiley.

Gavey, N. 2005. *Just Sex? The Cultural Scaffolding of Rape.* New York: Routledge.

Gaylord, M. S., and J. F. Galliher. 1988. *The Criminology of Edwin Sutherland.* New Brunswick, NJ: Transaction Books.

Giddens, A. 1991. *Modernity and Self Identity.* Stanford, CA: Stanford University Press.

———. 1984. *The Constitution of Society.* Berkeley: University of California Press.

———. 1976. *New Rules of Sociological Method: A Positive Critique of Interpretive Sociologies.* New York: Basic Books.

Goetting, A. 1999. *Getting Out: Life Stories of Women Who Left Abusive Men.* New York: Columbia University Press.

Goffman, E. 1979. *Gender Advertisements.* New York: Harper & Row.

———. 1972. *Relations in Public.* New York: Harper & Row.

———. 1968. *Stigma.* Englewood Cliffs, NJ: Prentice-Hall.

———. 1963. *Behavior in Public Places.* New York: Free Press.

Gottfredson, M. R., and T. Hirschi. 1990. *A General Theory of Crime.* Stanford, CA: Stanford University Press.

Hirschfield, M. 1922. *Homosexuality of Men and Women.* New York: Prometheus Books.

Hirschi, T. 1969. *Causes of Delinquency.* Berkeley, CA: University of California Press.

Hollway, W. 1984. "Women's Power in Heterosexual Sex." *Women's Studies International Forum* 7 (1): 63–68.

Holstein, J. A., and J. F. Gubrium. 1995. *The Active Interview.* Thousand Oaks, CA: Sage.

Hooton, E. A. 1939a. *The American Criminal.* Cambridge, MA: Harvard University Press.

———. 1939b. *Crime and the Man.* Cambridge, MA: Harvard University Press.

Horn, D. 2003. *The Criminal Body: Lombroso and the Anatomy of Deviance.* New York: Routledge.

Jackson, S. 2007. "The Sexual Self in Late Modernity." In M. Kimmel, ed. *The Sexual Self: The Construction of Sexual Scripts*, 3–15. Nashville, TN: Vanderbilt University Press.

Jackson, S., and S. Scott. 2010. *Theorizing Sexuality*. New York: McGraw-Hill.

Kessler, S. 1990. "The Medical Construction of Gender: Case Management of Intersexed Infants." *Signs: Journal of Women in Culture and Society* 16 (1): 3–26.

Kessler, S., and W. McKenna. 1978. *Gender: An Ethnomethodological Approach*. New York: John Wiley.

Kimmel, M. S. 2005. *The Gender of Desire*. Albany, NY: SUNY Press.

Kimmel, M. S., and M. Mahler. 2003. "Adolescent Masculinity, Homophobia, and Violence: Random School Shootings, 1982–2001." *American Behavioral Scientist* 46 (10): 1439–58.

Kindlon, D., and M. Thompson. 1999. *Raising Cain: Protecting the Emotional Life of Boys*. New York: Ballantine.

Kinsey, A., W. H. Pomeroy, and C. E. Martin. 1948. *Sexual Behavior in the Human Male*. Philadelphia: W. B. Sanders.

Kinsey, A., W. H. Pomeroy, C. E. Martin, and P. H. Gebhard. 1953. *Sexual Behavior in the Human Female*. Philadelphia: W. B. Sanders.

Kitzinger, C. 2005a. "Heteronormativity in Action: Reproducing the Heterosexual Nuclear Family in After-Hours Medical Calls." *Social Problems* 52 (4): 477–98.

———. 2005b. "'Speaking as a Heterosexual': (How) Does Sexuality Matter for Talk-in-Interaction?" *Research on Language and Social Interaction* 38 (3): 221–65.

Klein, J. 2011. *The Bully Society*. New York: New York University Press.

Kobrin, S. 1982. "The Uses of the Life-History Document for the Development of Delinquency Theory." In J. Snodgrass, ed. *The Jack Roller at Seventy*, 153–65. Lexington, MA: Lexington Books.

Krafft-Ebing, R. 1886. *Sexual Psychopathy: A Clinical-Forensic Study*. New York: Putnam.

Laqueur, T. 1990. *Making Sex: Body and Gender from the Greeks to Freud*. Cambridge, MA: Harvard University Press.

Laub, J. H., and R. J. Sampson. 1991. "The Sutherland-Glueck Debate: On the Sociology of Criminological Knowledge." *American Journal of Sociology* 96 (6): 1402–40.

Leonard, E. B. 1982. *Women, Crime, and Society: A Critique of Criminological Theory*. New York: Longman.

Lipton, S. 2011. "Those Manly Men of Yore." *New York Times*, June 17, A35.

Lombroso, C. 1876. *L'uomo delinquente*. Milan: Hoepl.

Lombroso, C., and G. Ferrero. 1893. (2004) *Criminal Woman, the Prostitute, and the Normal Woman*. Translated and introduced by N. H. Rafter and M. Gibson. Durham, NC: Duke University Press.

Lorber, J., and L. A. Moore. 2007. *Gendered Bodies: Feminist Perspectives*. Los Angeles: Roxbury.

Lumeng, J., P. Forrest, D. Appugliese, N. Kaciroti, R. Corwyn, and R. Bradley. 2010. "Weight Status as a Predictor of Being Bullied in Third through Sixth Grades." *Pediatrics* 125 (6): 1301–7.

Maher, L. 1997. *Sexed Work: Gender, Race, and Resistance in a Brooklyn Drug Market*. New York: Oxford University Press.

Martin, P. Y. 2003. "'Said and Done' Versus 'Saying and Doing': Gendering Practices, Practicing Gender at Work." *Gender and Society* 17 (3): 342–66.

Martin, S. E., and N. C. Jurik. 2007. *Doing Justice, Doing Gender: Women in Law and Criminal Justice Occupations*. Thousand Oaks, CA: Sage.

Mead, G. H. 1967. *Mind, Self and Society*. Chicago: University of Chicago Press.

Merten, D. 1997. "The Meaning of Meanness: Popularity, Competition, and Conflict among Junior High School Girls." *Sociology of Education* 70 (1): 175–91.

Messerschmidt, J. W. 2010. *Hegemonic Masculinities and Camouflaged Politics: Unmasking the Bush Dynasty and Its War against Iraq*. Boulder, CO: Paradigm.

———. 2008. "And Now, the Rest of the Story . . ." *Men and Masculinities* 11 (1): 83–101.

———. 2004. *Flesh and Blood: Adolescent Gender Diversity and Violence*. Lanham, MD: Rowman & Littlefield.

———. 2000. *Nine Lives: Adolescent Masculinities, the Body, and Violence*. Boulder, CO: Westview.

———. 1997. *Crime as Structured Action: Gender, Race, Class, and Crime in the Making*. Thousand Oaks, CA: Sage.

———. 1993. *Masculinities and Crime: Critique and Reconceptualization of Theory*. Lanham, MD: Rowman & Littlefield.

———. 1986. *Capitalism, Patriarchy, and Crime*. Totowa, NJ: Rowman & Littlefield.

Meyer, E. J. 2009. *Gender, Bullying, and Harassment*. New York: Teachers College Press.

Miller, J. 2008. *Getting Played: African American Girls, Urban Inequality, and Gendered Violence.* New York: New York University Press.

———. 2002. "The Strengths and Limits of 'Doing Gender' for Understanding Street Crime." *Theoretical Criminology* 6 (4): 433–60.

———. 2001. *One of the Guys: Girls, Gangs, and Gender.* New York: Oxford University Press.

Morgan, D. 1992. *Discovering Men.* New York: Routledge.

Morgan, D., and S. Scott, eds. 1993. *Body Matters: Essays on the Sociology of the Body.* Washington, DC: Falmer Press.

Mullins, C. 2006. *Holding Your Square: Masculinities, Street Life, and Violence.* Portland, OR: Willan.

Naffine, N., ed. 1995. *Gender, Crime, and Feminism.* Brookfield, VT: Dartmouth.

Naffine, N. 1987. *Female Crime: The Construction of Women in Criminology.* Sydney: Allen & Unwin.

National Center for Education Statistics. 2008. *Indicators of School Crime and Safety, 2007.* Washington, DC: National Center for Education Statistics.

Neal, D. G. 2008. *The Masculine Self in Late Medieval England.* Chicago: University of Chicago Press.

Newburn, T., and E. A. Stanko, eds. 1994. *Just Boys Doing Business? Men, Masculinities and Crime.* London: Routledge.

Oakley, A. 1972. *Sex, Gender and Society.* San Francisco: Harper & Row.

Orbuch, T. 1997. "People's Accounts Count: The Sociology of Accounts." In J. Hagan and K. S. Cook, eds. *Annual Review of Sociology* 23, 455–78. Palo Alto, CA: Annual Reviews, Inc.

Owens, L., and N. Duncan. 2009. "'They Might Not Like you but Everyone Knows You': Popularity among Teenage Girls." *Journal of Student Wellbeing* 3 (1): 14–39.

Padfield, M., and I. Procter. 1996. "The Effect of Interviewer's Gender on the Interviewing Process: A Comparative Study." *Sociology* 30 (2): 35–66.

Patton, M. Q. 1990. *Qualitative Evaluation and Research Methods.* Newbury Park, CA: Sage.

Perry, D., E. Hodges, and S. Egan. 2001. "Determinants of Chronic Victimization by Peers: A Review and New Model of Family Influence." In J. Juvonan and S. Graham, eds. *Peer Harassment in School: The Plight of the Vulnerable and Victimized,* 73–104. New York: Guildford.

Peterson, A. 2011. "The 'Long Winding Road' to Adulthood: A Risk-Filled Journey for Young People in Stockholm's Marginalized Periphery." *Young* 19 (3): 271–89.

Plummer, K. 2001. *Documents of Life II: An Invitation to Critical Humanism.* Thousand Oaks, CA: Sage.

Polk, K. 1994. *When Men Kill: Scenarios of Masculine Violence.* New York: Cambridge University Press.

Pollak, O. 1950. *The Criminality of Women.* New York: A. S. Barnes.

Presser, L. 2008. *Been a Heavy Life: Stories of Violent Men.* Urbana, IL: University of Illinois Press.

Pronk, R. E., and M. J. Zimmer-Gembeck. 2010. "It's 'Mean,' But What Does It Mean to Adolescents? Relational Aggression Described by Victims, Aggressors, and Their Peers." *Journal of Adolescent Research* 25 (2): 175–204.

Rafter, N. H., and M. Gibson. 2004. "Editors' Introduction." In C. Lombroso and G. Ferrero, *Criminal Woman, the Prostitute, and the Normal Woman,* 3–33. Durham, NC: Duke University Press.

Rafter, N. H., and F. Heidensohn. 1995. "Introduction: The Development of Feminist Perspectives on Crime." In N. H. Rafter and F. Heidensohn, eds. *International Feminist Perspectives in Criminology: Engendering a Discipline,* 1–14. Philadelphia: Open University Press.

Reinhartz, S. 1992. *Feminist Methods in Social Research.* New York: Oxford University Press.

Reynolds, B. M., and R. L. Repetti. 2010. "Teenage Girls' Perceptions of the Functions of Relationally Aggressive Behaviors." *Psychology in the Schools* 47 (3): 282–96.

Richardson, L. 1990. *Writing Strategies: Reaching Diverse Audiences.* Newbury Park, CA: Sage.

Rigby, K. 2002. *New Perspectives on Bullying.* Philadelphia: Jessica Kingsley.

Righthand, S., and C. Welch. 2005. "Characteristics of Youth Who Sexually Offend." *Journal of Child Sexual Abuse* 13 (3/4): 15–32.

Rose, A., L. Swenson, and E. Waller. 2004. "Overt Relational Aggression and Perceived Popularity: Developmental Differences in Concurrent and Prospective Relations." *Developmental Psychology* 40 (3): 378–87.

Sabo, D., T. A. Kupers, W. London, eds. 2001. *Prison Masculinities.* Philadelphia: Temple University Press.

Salisbury, J., and D. Jackson. 1996. *Challenging Macho Values: Practical Ways of Working with Adolescent Boys.* London: Falmer Press.

Sampson, R. J., and J. H. Laub. 1993. *Crime in the Making: Pathways and Turning Points Through Life.* Cambridge: Harvard University Press.

Sartre, J. P. 1963. *Search for a Method*. New York: Alfred A. Knopf.
———. 1956. *Being and Nothingness*. New York: Washington Square Press.
Schippers, M. 2007. "Recovering the Feminine Other: Masculinity, Femininity, and Gender Hegemony." *Theory & Society* 36 (1): 85–102.
Schwendinger, H., and J. Schwendinger. 1983. *Rape and Inequality*. Beverly Hills, CA: Sage.
Schwartz, B. K., D. Cavanaugh, A. Pimental, and R. Prentky. 2006. "Descriptive Study of Precursors to Sex Offending among 813 Boys and Girls: Antecedent Life Experiences." *Victims and Offenders* 1 (1): 61–77.
Seidman, I. 1998. *Interviewing as Qualitative Research*. New York: Teachers College Press.
Seidman, S. 2010. *The Social Construction of Sexuality*. 2nd ed. New York: Norton.
Shaw, C. 1930. *The Jack Roller*. Chicago: University of Chicago Press.
Shaw, C. R., and H. McKay. 1929. *Delinquency Areas*. Chicago: University of Chicago Press.
Sheldon, W. H. 1949. *Varieties of Delinquent Youth*. New York: Harper.
Shilling, C. 2003. *The Body and Social Theory*. Thousand Oaks, CA: Sage.
Short, J. F. 1982. "Life History, Autobiography, and the Life Cycle." In J. Snodgrass, ed. *The Jack Roller at Seventy*, 135–52. Lexington, MA: Lexington Books.
Smart, C. 1989. *Feminism and the Power of Law*. New York: Routledge.
Stanko, E. 1985. *Intimate Intrusions: Women's Experience of Male Violence*. Boston: Routledge & Kegan Paul.
Strauss, A., and J. Corbin. 1998. *Basics of Qualitative Research*. Thousand Oaks, CA: Sage.
Sutherland, E. H. 1956. "Development of the Theory." In K. Schuessler, ed. *Edwin H. Sutherland: On Analyzing Crime*, 13–29. Chicago: University of Chicago Press.
———. 1950. "The Sexual Psychopath Laws." *Journal of Criminal Law and Criminology* 40 (5): 543–54.
———. 1947. *Principles of Criminology*. Philadelphia: Lippincott.
———. 1939. *Principles of Criminology*. Philadelphia: Lippincott.
———. 1937. *The Professional Thief*. Chicago: University of Chicago Press.
———. 1932. "Social Process in Behavior Problems." *Publications of the American Sociological Society* 26: 55–61.
———. 1926. "The Biological and Sociological Processes." *Papers and Proceedings of the Twentieth Annual Meeting of the American Sociological Society* 20: 58–65.

————. 1924. *Criminology*. Philadelphia: Lippincott.

Sweeting, H., and P. West. 2001. "Being Different: Correlates of the Experience of Teasing and Bullying at Age 11." *Research Papers in Education* 16: 225–46.

Theoretical Criminology. 2002. 6 (1).

Thomas, W. I., and F. Znaniecki. (1927) 1958. *The Polish Peasant in Europe and America*. New York: Dover.

Thrasher, F. M. 1927. *The Gang: A Study of 1,313 Gangs in Chicago*. Chicago: University of Chicago Press.

Tomsen, S. 2009. *Violence, Prejudice and Sexuality*. New York: Routledge.

Tomsen, S., ed. 2008. *Crime, Criminal Justice, and Masculinities*. Burlington, VT: Ashgate.

Turner, B. S. 1996. *The Body and Society: Explorations in Social Theory*. 2nd ed. Thousand Oaks, CA: Sage.

Vick, J., R. McRoy, and B. M. Matthews. 2002. "Young Female Sex Offenders: Assessment and Treatment Issues." *Journal of Child Sexual Abuse* 11 (2): 1–23.

Wacquant, L. 2004. *Body & Soul: Notebooks of an Apprentice Boxer*. New York: Oxford University Press.

West, C., and S. Fenstermaker. 1995. "Doing Difference." *Gender and Society* 9 (1): 8–37.

West, C., and D. H. Zimmerman. 1987. "Doing Gender." *Gender and Society* 1 (2): 125–51.

Williams, C. L., and E. J. Heikes. 1993. "The Importance of Researcher's Gender in the In-Depth Interview: Evidence from Two Case Studies of Male Nurses." *Gender and Society* 7 (2): 280–91.

Winlow, S. 2001. *Badfellas: Crime, Tradition and New Masculinities*. New York: Berg.

Witz, A. 2000. "Whose Body Matters? Feminist Sociology and the Corporeal Turn in Sociology and Feminism." *Body and Society* 6 (2): 1–24.

Witz, A., and B. Marshall. 2003. "The Quality of Manhood: Masculinity and Embodiment in the Sociological Tradition." *The Sociological Review* 51 (31): 339–56.

Young, I. M. 1990. *Throwing Like a Girl and Other Essays in Feminist Philosophy and Social Theory*. Bloomington: Indiana University Press.

Zolondek, S. O., G. G. Abel, W. F. Northey, and A. D. Jordan. 2003. "The Self-Reported Behaviors of Juvenile Sex Offenders." In C. Hensley and R. Tewksbury, eds. *Sexual Deviance: A Reader*, 119–29. Boulder, CO: Lynne Rienner.

Index

CPSIA information can be obtained at www.ICGtesting.com
Printed in the USA
BVOW032240240213

314000BV00003B/7/P